PENGUIN PASSNOTES

The Merchant of Venice

D0671534

Peter Millson was educated at King's College School,
Wimbledon, and University College, Oxford. After
graduating, he remained in Oxford, teaching English
Language and Literature in a tutorial college. He now
lives and works in London.

PENGUIN PASSNOTES

WILLIAM SHAKESPEARE

The Merchant of Venice

PETER MILLSON

ADVISORY EDITOR: STEPHEN COOTE M.A., PH.D

PENGUIN BOOKS

PENGUIN BOOKS

Published by the Penguin Group
Penguin Books Ltd, 27 Wrights Lane, London W8 5TZ, England
Viking Penguin, a division of Penguin Books USA Inc.
375 Hudson Street, New York, New York 10014, USA
Penguin Books Australia Ltd, Ringwood, Victoria, Australia
Penguin Books Canada Ltd, 2801 John Street, Markham, Ontario, Canada L3R 1B4
Penguin Books (NZ) Ltd, 182–190 Wairau Road, Auckland 10, New Zealand

Penguin Books Ltd, Registered Offices: Harmondsworth, Middlesex, England

First published 1984
10 9 8 7 6 5

Printed in England by Clays Ltd, St Ives plc
Filmset in Monophoto Ehrhardt

Contents

To the Student

This book is designed to help you with your GCSE English Literature examinations. It contains an introduction to the play, analysis of scenes and characters, and a commentary on some of the issues raised by the play. Line references are to the New Penguin Shakespeare, edited by W. Moelwyn Merchant.

When you use this book remember that it is no more than an aid to your study. It will help you find passages quickly and perhaps give you some ideas for essays. But remember: *This book is not a substitute for reading the play and it is your response and your knowledge that matter*. These are the things the examiners are looking for, and they are also the things that will give you the most pleasure. Show your knowledge and appreciation to the examiner, and show them clearly.

Introduction: Background to The Merchant of Venice

The age of Shakespeare saw the emergence of a new, broadly based, European culture. Englishmen began to travel, and became aware of the outside world. For Shakespeare and his audience, a knowledge of the world and accomplishments in language and literature became almost as important attributes for success as good birth. This blossoming of new learning and new horizons is mirrored in the various settings of Shakespeare's plays: Rome, Athens, Vienna, Milan and Venice. It is personified by the wits and gallants who populate the plays. It can be heard in their language, which had been hugely enriched from both classical and foreign sources. The characters, language and setting of *The Merchant of Venice* all show how Shakespeare played a part in this new and exciting culture.

Drama was the most popular literary form in Shakespeare's time. It appealed to a public accustomed to listening rather than reading, to a shared life rather than solitary pastimes. The characters in *The Merchant of Venice* turn to masques and music for their entertainment, sharing this powerful sense of community with their audience.

The fortunes of a rich merchant like Antonio would have immediately appealed to an Elizabethan audience. Although most people still lived in the country, rather than in towns, and worked the land, the prosperity of the nation was to some extent dependent on trade. This had flourished on a broad, international scale. The life of the merchant classes and the adventures and dangers of sea voyages were a natural preoccupation for dramatists and audiences alike. Venice was seen by all as the city most representative of a prosperous merchant society. In the popular imagination it was a place of fabulous wealth, royal merchants, richly attired gentlemen and refined culture. Shakespeare tried to show all of these aspects in his play.

However, despite the new wealth of the age, many aristocrats fell deeply into debt and found it impossible to reduce their expenses or accept a more austere way of life. In *The Merchant of Venice*, Bassanio discovers that the only solution to such a problem is to turn to the money-lenders.

Usury – the lending of money at exorbitant rates of interest – was legalized in England in 1571, but almost all of Shakespeare's contemporaries strongly disapproved of it. They considered usury to be bad for the economy and an immoral activity. Many books and pamphlets were published on the controversial subject, and the debate was also reflected in the drama of the period. Through Antonio, Shakespeare echoes this general condemnation.

Jews, who were considered to be the greediest and the worst usurers, were subject to a great deal of racial hatred in Shakespeare's England, although they were few in number at the time. Perhaps their rarity made them seem even more suspect. At any rate, the word 'Jew' was often synonymous with miser or money-lender, and this is how they were invariably characterized in contemporary drama. Complete with false nose and beard, the actors who played such roles as Pisaro, in Haughton's *Englishmen for My Money*, or Zariph, in Day's *Travels of Three English Gentlemen*, portrayed characters without a single redeeming feature. Perhaps the most famous Jew of all the dramatic literature of the age was Barabas in Marlowe's *The Jew of Malta*. Such Jews of popular drama were all portrayed as greedy, vile and vicious. How does Shylock fit in with this? We shall see (pp. 50–57) that Shakespeare was somewhat more sophisticated than these other writers in the presentation of his stage Jew. He focuses his audience's attention on a particular Jew rather than on Jews as a whole, but he does, nonetheless, exploit the comic potential of the type just as his contemporaries had done. In *The Merchant of Venice* jokes abound about the Jews being devils and devourers of Christian flesh.

The readiness of the public to relish all this is well illustrated by an incident that occurred in 1594, not long before *The Merchant of Venice* was written. A Jew named Lopez – no less a man than the Queen's doctor – was tried for conspiracy against her life. Racial prejudice was even drawn into the courtroom when the judges referred to 'that vile Jew'. The presentation of Shylock is to some extent a product of this atmosphere. The Shylock Shakespeare depicts is a wholly Elizabethan Jew, and we shall see that many other themes in the play deal with problems of particular relevance to Shakespeare's audience. Thus, although Shakespeare's work has come to be regarded as a timeless monument to poetry, it must also be remembered that he was a popular dramatist with an eye for the interests and moods of his audience.

Synopsis

In Act I Scene i we are introduced to Antonio, the wealthy merchant of Venice from whom the play takes its title. He is conversing with two gallants named Salerio and Solanio. Antonio is gripped by a melancholy he cannot understand, but his two friends are sure they know the reason for it: he is worried because all his assets are on the high seas, and have not yet safely reached their destinations. Antonio's great business venture is central to the plot, but he denies that this is the reason for his low spirits. Bassanio then enters with Lorenzo and Gratiano; he has been looking for Antonio, and the others leave them together to talk. Bassanio wants to borrow money from Antonio to enable him to go to Belmont to woo Portia, a beautiful heiress whom he greatly admires. He is already deeply in debt to Antonio but suggests that if Antonio agrees to a further loan he will stand a good chance of recovering the money he has already lent, since Portia is extremely rich. Antonio is more than willing to help, but because his money is all tied up he has nothing to lend. He therefore advises Bassanio to try to borrow from someone else. He does offer to guarantee the loan, however, and this is crucial.

The scene moves to Portia's home in Belmont. We find her talking to her waiting woman, Nerissa (Act I Scene ii). Portia seems discontented with the terms of her father's will, which specify how her husband will be chosen. There are three caskets – one gold, one silver, and one lead – and whoever selects the right one will win Portia's hand in marriage. Those who choose wrongly, as we later learn, must swear that they will never marry and leave Belmont forthwith.

Many suitors are already courting Portia. Nerissa names each suitor in turn, but Portia gives good reasons for disliking all of them. Fortunately none of the suitors is prepared to accept her father's conditions and they all leave. Nerissa reminds her mistress of when she met Bassanio, and both agree he is a true gentleman. Finally, a messenger enters to announce the arrival of yet another hopeful suitor – the Prince of Morocco.

We return to Venice and meet Shylock for the first time (Act I Scene iii). Bassanio is applying to him for a loan of three thousand ducats for three months. Shylock is prepared to accept Antonio's bond for the amount. When Antonio arrives, Shylock, in an aside to the audience, expresses his hatred for him. He has been scorned and insulted because he is a Jew and longs for a chance to get even with the Venetian gentiles. After a heated exchange and a show of mutual animosity, Antonio exhorts Shylock to lend the money as he would to an enemy, and to exact the penalty without qualms if the loan is not repaid on time. Seizing his opportunity, Shylock pretends that he really wants the young man's friendship and, as a token of his supposedly kind intentions, proposes the terms of the bond by which he secretly hopes to destroy Antonio. He will demand no interest. Instead, if the agreement is broken, the forfeit will be a pound of Antonio's flesh. Antonio is convinced that Shylock is only joking, and he dismisses Bassanio's misgivings, saying that his ships will be safely home a month before repayment of the loan is due.

At the beginning of the second Act we return to Belmont. The Prince of Morocco has now arrived, and is very anxious: he would risk his life to win Portia, but he is reluctant to chance everything on choosing the right casket. However, he determines to try his luck.

His choice is temporarily delayed as Shakespeare returns to Venice to introduce us to Shylock's servant, Launcelot Gobbo, the clown (Act II Scene ii). He is in the midst of a furious debate with himself, after which he decides to leave Shylock's household. His father, Old Gobbo, then appears, looking for Launcelot. He is so blind that he does not recognize his son, who has some fun at the old man's expense before admitting his identity. Launcelot then explains his plan to desert Shylock, and enlists Old Gobbo's help in entering Bassanio's service. At this point Bassanio enters and agrees to employ Launcelot, who departs to take his leave of Shylock. Gratiano then arrives, and Bassanio agrees to let him accompany him to Belmont.

Meanwhile, Launcelot is bidding farewell to Shylock's daughter, Jessica (Act II Scene iii). She is as keen as Launcelot to leave Shylock, and we learn that she intends to do so by eloping with her lover, Lorenzo. She gives Launcelot a note to take to him.

In the next scene, Lorenzo and his friends are preparing a masque to enhance the evening's feast, and after he has received Jessica's message and entrusted Launcelot with a reply, Lorenzo confides in Gratiano that Jessica will make good her escape that evening disguised as Lorenzo's torchbearer in the masque. We also discover that she is going to steal gold and jewels from her father.

Launcelot returns to Shylock's house to invite him, on behalf of his new master, Bassanio, to the feast (Act II Scene v). He secretly tells Jessica that Lorenzo will be coming to collect her, as planned. Shylock reluctantly accepts the invitation and leaves the house, thereby giving Jessica her chance to escape. In Act II Scene vi, the masquers await Lorenzo outside Shylock's house. Jessica appears at the upstairs window, somewhat embarrassed by her page-boy disguise, but, having furnished herself with more of her father's money, she descends, and the young people leave to perform the masque. Gratiano is about to follow them but is intercepted by Antonio, who tells him that the celebrations have been curtailed. Bassanio has decided to make the most of a favourable wind and set sail for Belmont at once.

Now, at last, we find ourselves back in Belmont and about to discover the fate of the Prince of Morocco. This is the first of three set-pieces devoted to the theme of the three caskets (Act II Scene vii). One of the caskets, we are told, contains a portrait of Portia. This is the casket the successful suitor must choose. Each one also bears an inscription. After considerable thought, Morocco selects the golden one which reads: 'Who chooseth me shall gain what many men desire'. He is sure this must refer to Portia herself, but all the casket contains is a death's-head and a scornful lyric. Morocco sorrowfully departs.

All the action up to this point is contained within a single day.

Back in Venice, Salerio and Solanio relate Shylock's almost comic bewilderment on discovering the double loss of his daughter and his ducats (Act II Scene viii). They are amused, but they are also fearful of the consequences for Antonio, especially as Salerio has heard of a richly laden vessel from Venice which has been wrecked. They suspect it is one of Antonio's, and are convinced that Shylock will claim his pound of flesh if he gets the chance.

Act II Scene ix contains the second of the casket scenes. This time the suitor is the proud Prince of Arragon, who picks the silver casket with the inscription: 'Who chooseth me shall get as much as he deserves'. However, on opening it he finds only a fool's head and another mocking lyric. He too leaves. A messenger enters announcing the imminent arrival of a Venetian lord. Nerissa voices the hope that it may be Bassanio.

Solanio opens the third Act with confirmation that Antonio has indeed lost one ship. Shylock enters and, in his famous speech of self-justification, swears that he will now take his revenge on Antonio. Tubal, another Jew, now joins him. He has been looking for Jessica but has failed to find her. In the course of his travels, however, he has gathered sufficient evidence to confirm Antonio's financial ruin.

In the meantime, Bassanio has arrived at Belmont (Act III Scene ii) for the last, and most important, of the casket scenes. He and Portia are already in love, and she wants him to postpone his choice in case he fails. However, Bassanio cannot bear the suspense and determines to proceed. To a prelude of a romantic and wistful speech from Portia, and a background of music, he deliberates at length over the inscriptions. Portia is ecstatic when Bassanio selects the lead casket, whose inscription reads: 'Who chooseth me must give and hazard all he hath', and finds her portrait inside. She gives him the ring which will be an object of some controversy at the end of the play, and Bassanio swears that he will never part with it. As we shall see, he fails to keep this promise. Gratiano and Nerissa complete the joyful, romantic mood by announcing their own plans to marry, but the general air of happiness is soon shattered when Lorenzo, Jessica and Salerio arrive, bearing the news of Antonio's bankruptcy. All his ships have been lost, and Bassanio explains to Portia the extent both of his debt and of the danger his friend is in. She urges him to leave for Venice as soon as they have been married, declaring her readiness to pay the debt to Shylock many times over.

Antonio has been arrested (Act I I I Scene iii). Solanio cannot believe that the Duke will enforce the terms of the bond, but Antonio is sure that he will be obliged to uphold the law. However, Portia has a plan. She tells Lorenzo and Jessica that she will await Bassanio's return in a monastery, but when they leave we discover her real intentions (Act I I I Scene iv). A letter is dispatched to her cousin, Doctor Bellario, and the messenger is told to meet her and Nerissa by the ferry to Venice, bringing notes and garments supplied by Bellario. Portia describes with relish how they will join their husbands without their knowledge, disguised as young men. She promises to explain everything to Nerissa as they travel to the ferry, but the audience has to wait a little longer to discover the exact details of her plan. The Act closes with a comic exchange between Launcelot, Jessica and Lorenzo, all of whom have remained in Belmont.

The vitally important scene of Antonio's trial occupies almost the whole of the fourth Act. Shylock is summoned to the court, and the Duke urges him to relent. He is unmoved even when Bassanio, who, as a result of his marriage, is now a rich man, offers to pay him twice his original loan. We then learn that the Duke has requested Portia's cousin, Bellario, to judge the case, and when Nerissa enters disguised as the clerk of a doctor of law, the full audacity of Portia's plan is revealed to the audience. Whilst Gratiano rails at Shylock, the Duke reads a letter from Bellario which Nerissa has given him. It says that he is too ill to attend, but that he has sent in his place a learned young doctor to give judgement. This young man, as the audience expects, is Portia in disguise.

Portia, like the Duke, implores Shylock to be merciful. He will not hear of this, and Antonio is told to prepare himself for death. Shylock is on the point of cutting into his flesh, when Portia confounds him with a legal quibble. He may take his pound of flesh, but if a drop of Antonio's blood is spilled Shylock will lose both his life and his wealth. In accordance with the laws of Venice, for an alien even to intend to injure one of its citizens is a crime. The punishment is that half the offender's wealth should go to the intended victim and the other half to the state. The Duke may also decide whether or not Shylock is to be allowed to live. In the event, Shylock's life is spared, and it is proposed that a fine should be substituted for the state's half of his property. The other half Antonio will have in trust, to be given to Lorenzo and Jessica along with the rest of Shylock's estate when he dies. In addition, Shylock must become a Christian. In despair, Shylock, with very little option, assents.

Bassanio offers the disguised Portia the three thousand ducats which she had given him to repay the loan. She refuses this, but when pressed to accept something as a token of Bassanio's gratitude insists on having the ring with which she made Bassanio promise never to part. At first Bassanio is true to his word, but when Antonio remonstrates with him he sends Gratiano after Portia with the ring. In Act IV Scene ii it is duly delivered, and Nerissa joins in the game by whispering to Portia that she will attempt to persuade Gratiano to part with the ring that she has also given him, and which he has similarly sworn to keep for ever. The women plan to leave that night in order to be at Belmont before their husbands return.

The audience arrives there before any of them (Act V Scene i). Lorenzo and Jessica are engaged in a beautiful, playful and romantic conversation in a grove in front of the house. Messengers enter announcing that Portia and Bassanio will soon be home. Portia and Nerissa arrive first, and tell the young lovers not to reveal their absence to their husbands, who enter almost immediately, accompanied by Antonio. They receive a warm welcome, but we soon discover that Nerissa was successful in obtaining her ring, for she begins playfully to rebuke Gratiano, saying that she is convinced he has given the ring to another woman. Bassanio is likewise forced to confess his misdeed, but he swears never to break his promise again. Once more Antonio secures the pledge, this time with his soul as the forfeit. At last Portia admits her deception, giving Antonio a letter from Bellario which not only reveals the identities of the young doctor and his clerk, but, in an outrageous *coup de théâtre*, also informs Antonio that three of his ships have miraculously arrived safely at their destinations. We leave the characters relishing their good fortune at the turn of events. The last words go to Gratiano, with his thoughts of the marriage-bed.

Scene by Scene Analysis

ACT I SCENE i

It may seem strange that a comedy should begin with a gloomy declaration of melancholy, boredom and confusion, (ll.1–7). Of course, the word 'comedy', when applied to one of Shakespeare's plays, does not imply a work simply intended to make you laugh. It carries associations of magic and romance, of a world sometimes reminiscent of a fairy-tale, in which happy endings, and the marriage of the hero and heroine, are assured. 'Comedy' in Shakespeare's plays denotes a highly artificial and contrived literary form. However, the characters that populate Shakespeare's comedies are far from immune to the darker elements of life. Here, Antonio's vague discontent anticipates the much more dangerous threat to his wellbeing presented by Shylock.

So, in *The Merchant of Venice*, and especially in those scenes set in Belmont, Shakespeare creates a privileged and idealized world. He also shows the fragility of this comic world. The audience enjoys the beauty and fun of romantic episodes, but at the same time is aware of a far more complex, unpleasant and constant threat outside of this easy existence. This feeling of vulnerability is vividly present in the opening conversation between Antonio, Salerio and Solanio.

Antonio's friends are convinced his mood is due to the fact that most of his wealth is bound up in his ships at sea. Salerio describes Antonio's ships, as 'signors and rich burghers on the flood' (l.10). Rocking in the wake of Antonio's vessels, other ships seem to 'curtsy to them' (l.13). The image conveys an idea of the ceremonial and social function of wealth – the ships behave like courteous merchants. This will be an important theme in the play. In contrast, Solanio stresses the risk involved in such a 'venture', and Salerio picks up the point: ships are at the mercy of the wind and the rocks. Throughout the play, the dual imagery of sea and tempest is used to symbolize external forces over which man has no control. There is also a suggestion that Antonio's generosity of character increases his vulnerability. The sides of his vessels are 'gentle' (l.32), and just a touch from the rocks would be enough to scatter their valuable cargo into the sea.

Antonio dismisses the notion that his poor spirits are the result of anxiety about his merchandise. He points out that it is not all contained in one ship, and denies that his entire fortune is at risk. However, we shall see that the destruction of these vessels is enough to ruin him. He scorns, too, Solanio's suggestion that he is in love.

It has often been suggested that Antonio's melancholy arises from the knowledge that he may soon lose his best friend, Bassanio. He already knows that Bassanio has sworn a 'secret pilgrimage' (l.120) to woo a beautiful woman whom he has met only once before. Throughout the play Antonio remains something of an isolated figure; at the end he still stands apart from the crowd. With the exception of Launcelot, he is the only unmarried member of the happy group who take their places in the idealized setting of Belmont.

Even at the start, Antonio seems rather at odds with the happy, loquacious mood of those around him. Solanio's and Salerio's conversation is elegant and colourful, rich in figurative language and classical allusion. In contrast, Antonio's responses seem somewhat prosaic, although he is very gracious when they take their leave, as Bassanio, Lorenzo and Gratiano join him.

Gratiano rebukes Antonio for his sour face and his reticence, saying that he should not be like the sort of man who tries to appear very wise and deep simply by not saying anything (ll.88–99). However, Gratiano is cast as something of a buffoon. When Antonio compares the world to 'a stage where every man must play a part', Gratiano identifies himself as a clown by saying, 'Let me play the fool' (l.79), and both Antonio and Bassanio agree that Gratiano speaks 'an infinite deal of nothing' (l.114). Gratiano's frivolous nature cannot affect Antonio's mood. Clearly, the difficulties which the characters experience in the play are not to be solved merely by a determination to be cheerful.

An example of one of these serious problems soon emerges when

Gratiano and Lorenzo leave Bassanio and Antonio together. Bassanio is deeply in debt, mostly to Antonio himself. He has been living in a style which his 'faint means' (l.125) cannot support.

Nonetheless, much of their conversation highlights the positive themes of the play. Antonio's response to his friend's anxiety to settle his debts illustrates everything that is to be admired in his character. His generosity seems boundless (ll.138–9):

> *My purse, my person, my extremest means*
> *Lie all unlocked to your occasions.*

Bassanio has only to say that he needs help, and Antonio will feel obliged to do all he can (ll.158–60). This contrasts starkly with Shylock's feelings about the compulsion to show mercy to Antonio during the trial (I V, i, 181). Shylock's only conception of constraint lies in the law, whilst Antonio follows his heart rather than his head. Even though he has no money to hand, he is prepared to use his credit to raise a loan.

Bassanio's words also serve to emphasize the play's ideals of love and romance. His confidence in his ability to settle his debts by marrying the immensely wealthy heiress, Portia, is 'pure innocence' (l.145). To justify it he appropriately offers 'childhood proof' (ll.140–45). He describes Portia as an ideal of beauty, but loves her not only because she is fair, but because she has 'wondrous virtues' (l.163). The imagery of love and riches fuses. Portia's hair is like a 'golden fleece' (l.170), but Bassanio feels no need to be embarrassed by admitting that Portia's charms are increased by her wealth.

However, a modern audience may feel a little uneasy. Our attitudes towards fortune-hunters are far more disapproving than were those of the Elizabethans. The language seems to work in two ways. On the one hand Bassanio's words suggest that love and money may be compatible; on the other, they imply that he is not entirely averse to profiting financially from the relationship, an attitude which we would normally associate with Shylock. Bassanio's use of the word 'thrift' [profit] (l.175) heightens this impression. Ironically, love seems to produce a good rate of interest, just as money does for Shylock.

In the first scene, then, Shakespeare sets his plot in motion and presents some of the ideals of generosity, love and friendship with which much of the play is concerned. But he has also introduced an element of unease. The idealized world of comedy is seen to be under threat both from external forces – symbolized by the sea and tempest – and from internal dangers. When Bassanio describes his intentions to win Portia's hand as 'plots' (l.133) we learn that even the most sympathetic characters are not to be allowed the unquestioned perfection of the heroes and heroines of a fairy-tale, despite the protestation of 'pure innocence'. For all his genuine love for Portia, Bassanio *is* a fortune hunter.

ACT I SCENE ii

Belmont, Portia's home, is the setting for poetry, music and romance, a place where life seems charmed, and the painful intrusion of dark elements into the comic world is minimal. However, just as Antonio's opening speech was full of melancholy, so Portia introduces herself by complaining of weariness (ll.1–2). Nerissa, her waiting-woman, suggests that this is because having too much wealth can be as bad as being poor. The implication is not that money is irrelevant to happiness, since the play often characterizes wealth as a social blessing quite compatible with love, but rather that Portia has been excessively self-indulgent. Portia agrees but suggests that it is far easier to invent maxims than to live by them, and her speech emphasizes the power of exuberance and emotions over cold reasoning (ll.17–20). Like Antonio, she too follows the dictates of her heart, and is therefore very frustrated at not being free to choose her own husband because of the terms of her father's will. For the benefit of the audience, Nerissa explains the conditions (ll.26–9). Portia's father had devised a test involving three caskets of gold, silver and lead. Whoever chooses the right casket will win Portia's hand, but those who choose incorrectly must, we learn later, pay the stern price laid down in the conditions.

This highly artificial test is of ancient origin and is found in many folk tales. Here it is the focal point of almost all the scenes at Belmont, and carries us deeper into the contrived and enchanted world of comedy and romance. Portia seems irritated by it, although later (I I, ii, 41) she shares Nerissa's confidence in her father's wisdom. Nerissa even suggests that the stratagem is the result of divine guidance: 'holy men at their death have good inspirations' (ll.26–7). Her trust is rewarded in this scene, as the suitors who are currently courting Portia, and who are heartily despised to a man, all decide they are not prepared to take the risk, and so depart. It is as if there is a benevolent spirit at work at Belmont.

A contrast between the two locations in the play – Venice and Belmont – is thus established. In Venice, the characters are to some extent ruled by the harsh realities of life, by the cold world of business and by the workings of an indifferent and sometimes a cruel fate. In Belmont, such difficulties seem to evaporate in a fairy-tale setting. Such a contrast is heightened as Portia, unlike Antonio, soon casts off her weariness, overcoming it with a characteristic burst of energetic, witty conversation. As Nerissa mentions the name of each of the current batch of suitors, Portia dismisses them with contempt, but the tone of her speech is light-hearted, and the vitality and resilience of her mind striking. Although the focus of romantic attention in the play, she is no passive, delicate object of desire. She shows the characteristics of a long line of Shakespearean comic heroines: exuberance and mental agility embellished with an incisive sense of humour. So, she knows 'it is a sin to be a mocker' (l.53), but cannot resist mocking. She says of the Neapolitan Prince and Count Palatine: 'I had rather be married to a death's-head with a bone in his mouth' (ll.48–9), and she likes the young German 'Very vilely in the morning when he is sober and most vilely in the afternoon when he is drunk' (ll.79–80).

The first scene at Belmont closes with growing romantic expectations when Nerissa reminds her mistress of her meeting with Bassanio and of how much they both admired him. At this moment, a messenger arrives to announce the imminent arrival of another suitor, the Prince of Morocco. Portia cannot raise much enthusiasm for the meeting, but retains her sense of humour (ll.118–23).

ACT I SCENE iii

Once more in Venice, we are rudely brought down to earth by Shylock, as Bassanio tries to secure his loan. Colourful banter soon gives way to the language of business and cold calculation. The gulf between the two characters seems enormous. Bassanio's efforts to maintain the connection between friendship and money – 'Will you pleasure me?' (l.7) – do not impress Shylock. His almost mechanical responses are amusing, but also ominous. Such dehumanization of a character is a common device in comedy, but it also implies cruelty and moral degeneration. This last is well illustrated by Shylock's use of the word 'good' (l.12). For him 'good' refers not to someone's kindness and humanity, but only to his wealth (see pp. 77–9).

Significantly, Shylock stresses the threat to Antonio's fortune from the sea. Shylock is the embodiment of those elements in the play which are inhuman and cold. Note too the contrast between Salerio's poetical and elegant description of the dangers of sea travel (I, i, 22–36), and Shylock's fragmented, inelegant speech (ll.20–24). Shylock decides to lend the money, but when Bassanio invites him to dine so that he may speak with Antonio, he is portrayed as an intruder into the festive spirit of the play. He will do business with these gentiles, but will not eat, drink or pray with them. This is the main role of Shylock's position as a Jew in the play. He is an outsider in every sense.

Shylock's aside as Antonio enters (ll.37–48) is important, because it serves to prevent an excessively sentimental attitude towards him. His deep hatred of Antonio is vividly conveyed, and his lust for revenge (ll.42–3) gives the lie to those critics who suggest that Shylock would not have insisted on having his pound of flesh were it not for the fact that he is later robbed of money and his daughter by a friend of Antonio's. He hates Antonio because he is a Christian but, significantly, most of all because he lends money free, thereby reducing the rate of interest which other money-lenders, such as himself, can charge. Antonio despises usury. An Elizabethan audience would have been equally contemptuous. A modern audience might take it for granted; but the comparison between Antonio's generosity and Shylock's avarice survives the change in attitudes.

However, once again our acceptance of the simple ideals of the play is qualified. Just as Bassanio's romantic aspirations are mixed with a desire for profit, Antonio does not emerge from this scene with character unblemished. He may despise usury, but he is not above employing it when the need arises, and Shylock makes the most of this, reminding him of his professed superiority (ll.65–6):

> *Methoughts you said you neither lend nor borrow*
> *Upon advantage.*

He goes on to cite the biblical story of how Jacob managed to profit by his skill in breeding sheep, 'and he was blest' (l.85). Shylock makes gold and silver 'breed' (l.92), and suggests that the increase of money is likewise a blessing. Moreover, when he says that Jacob did not take 'Directly interest' (l.73), he is implying that there is more than one way to take interest. A modern audience at least might reflect that Antonio is a merchant and like all businessmen he trades for profit, which may be considered a form of indirect interest. So, although Antonio's and Shylock's characters are starkly contrasted in this scene, under the surface there are ominous hints of similarities between them. Antonio maintains that Jacob's fortune was the will of God, and cannot be compared to the profiteering of money-lenders, but it is not clear who has really won the argument.

Our discomfort is increased as Shylock describes how Antonio has treated him in the past. Antonio's hatred seems every bit as vicious as Shylock's. He has insulted him, spat at him, even kicked him like a dog, and there is a germ of potential tragedy as Shylock describes himself enduring this treatment 'with a patient shrug'. Shylock is thus in a strong position to taunt Antonio, and he exploits it to the full. If he is a dog, how can he lend three thousand ducats? (ll.117–18). This idea is developed later on in the play (III, iii, 7–8):

> *Thou call'dst me dog before thou hadst a cause,*
> *But since I am a dog, beware my fangs.*

He is suggesting that Antonio has only himself to blame for his position. Here, too, Antonio seems partly responsible for his own fate. Possibly stung by the element of truth in Shylock's accusations, it is

Antonio himself who suggests that Shylock should lend the money as he would 'to thine enemy' (l.131), imposing the usual terms of a loan. If the money is not repaid on time, Shylock should feel no qualms about exacting the penalty.

Hypocritically pretending to agree with Bassanio's and Antonio's ideas about money, Shylock proposes not to demand any interest, out of 'kindness' (l.139). Instead, if the loan is not repaid, he will cut off a pound of Antonio's flesh. He pretends that it is a joke, 'a merry sport' (l.141). We may wonder at Antonio's gullibility, but we can only admire his generosity of character: he is prepared to accept Shylock's offer at face value and dismisses Bassanio's all too justifiable misgivings.

Thus another major theme of the play is introduced: the difference between the appearance of things and reality; ironically, Antonio has anticipated it earlier on in the scene, when he says of Shylock, 'O what a goodly outside falsehood hath!' (l.98). Here the need to see beneath the surface is forcefully shown by Antonio's disastrous acceptance of Shylock's false 'kindness'. Later in the play it is Bassanio's ability not to discern purely by external appearances which enables him to win Portia.

ACT II SCENE i

The Prince of Morocco has arrived in Belmont, and his first speech gives a feeling of continuity, despite the change of location. He echoes the theme of the difference between appearance and reality by asking Portia not to judge him by his dark complexion. Underneath his skin, he says, his blood is redder than 'the fairest creature northward born' (l.4). Portia points out that the choice is at any rate not really hers to make. She shows tact in her speech, and, once again, her sense of humour. Morocco is reassured when she affirms that he is as fair as any of the suitors she has yet seen, but the audience shares her joke. The standard is, after all, not very high.

Morocco presents quite a striking figure. He is a 'tawny Moor all in white' (stage direction), and his language is rich and rhetorical. Indeed, he seems rather arrogant, boasting about his feats in battle and his courage (ll.24–31). However, he contemplates the test of the caskets with some trepidation, feeling (quite rightly) that his bravery and strength will be of little use to him in this test. He thinks that it is a question of pure luck, although in fact the riddle of the caskets is rather more subtle than that. We now learn something new about the conditions to which the suitors must adhere: each suitor must first swear that if he fails he will never marry at all (ll.40–42). In spite of all this, Morocco determines to try his luck. Portia plays the perfect hostess – Morocco will not make his choice until they have dined together.

ACT II SCENE ii

The contrast between Morocco's noble, elevated language and the comic verbosity of Launcelot Gobbo, the clown, could scarcely be greater. The effect is comic bathos: a descent from the sublime grandiloquence of Morocco to the ridiculous speech and behaviour of Launcelot. Here he is quite happy to carry out a fierce debate with himself. 'A fiend' is tempting him to leave Shylock, his master, but his conscience urges him to remain. The clown provides Shakespeare with a suitable mouthpiece for a contemptuous comic perspective of Shylock, in which he makes the common association of Jews with devils (a standard Elizabethan joke). Although to obey the fiend and leave Shylock would be tantamount to following the devil, to stay would be to live with an 'incarnation' of the devil (l.24). The conclusion is predictable: 'I will run' (l.28).

His father, Old Gobbo, enters. His eyesight is so poor that he does not immediately recognize his son. The situation is exploited principally for comic effect, but it is worth noting that their conversation sometimes touches light-heartedly on some of the main themes of the play. Perhaps there is an echo of Antonio's gullibility and inability to detect pretence in this ludicrous situation (see pp. 83–4). Old Gobbo is convinced by Launcelot that his son is dead, and then for a time refuses to believe him when he admits his identity. Again, their repeated malapropisms (ridiculous confusion between words) remind us of Antonio's far more dangerous misinterpretation of Shylock's 'kindness', and of Shylock's distortion of the word 'good'. Here Old Gobbo says 'infection' for 'affection', 'defect' for 'effect'; and Launcelot confuses 'frutify' with 'certify', and 'impertinent' with 'pertinent'.

Launcelot's affirmation that 'in the end truth will out' (l.74) is in harmony with the movement of Shakespeare's comedy: all conflicts and mistakes will eventually be happily resolved. Even in the most purely comic scenes, the continuity of the play is maintained. Launcelot emphasizes Shylock's miserliness, and in seeking to leave him to enter Bassanio's service he highlights the contrast between the two characters. Shylock may be rich, but Bassanio has 'the grace of God' (ll.138–9). By appreciating this distinction between material wealth and the richness of love, and by being an 'unthrifty knave' (I, iii, 171), Launcelot wins his job with Bassanio, and eventually his place in Belmont.

When Bassanio has agreed to take on Launcelot, he tells Leonardo to dispatch all business and be ready for the evening's feast. Once again we are reminded of the sociability of the Venetian way of life. These bonds of friendship are further emphasized when Gratiano enters, begging to be allowed to accompany Bassanio to Belmont. Bassanio agrees but tells him to mind his manners, for many things that are acceptable in Venice would be out of place in Belmont (ll.166–71). This sensitivity to the environment is an indispensable quality in Shakespearean comedy. It is partly because Shylock is so painfully at odds with the mood and atmosphere of the society in which he lives, and of the play itself, that he is confounded. Gratiano promises to moderate his behaviour, except during the festivities that night.

ACT II SCENE iii

Launcelot is saying farewell to Shylock's daughter, Jessica. She is very reluctant to see him go, since she considers 'Our house is hell' (l.2). Even his daughter characterizes Shylock as the devil. Launcelot, whom she good-humouredly calls a 'merry devil', was the only member of the household who relieved the tedium and introduced an element of the festivity which is the key note of the play. However, she does not intend to endure her present circumstances for long. She gives Launcelot a letter to take to Lorenzo, with whom she intends to elope and become a Christian. Lorenzo has promised to marry her. Even in this cameo scene we may admire the qualities of warmth and friendship which Shylock so manifestly lacks: there is a genuine affection in the parting of Launcelot and Jessica.

Jessica feels uncomfortable about her attitude towards her father, describing it as a 'heinous sin' (l.16). However, when Launcelot jokingly suggests that Shylock is not her real father, Jessica takes up the point: she may have Shylock's blood, but she has inherited none of his characteristics. Once again, the truth lies deeper than the superficial appearance of things. Jessica is Shylock's daughter and a Jewess, but in her heart she has more in common with the Christians.

ACT II SCENE iv

Lorenzo is discussing the arrangements for the masque which he and his friends plan to perform that evening. Solanio and Salerio, as socially polished and elegant as ever, are concerned that they have not yet arranged for torchbearers to accompany them, and feel that unless the thing is done properly, it would be better not to do it at all: 'Tis vile, unless it may be quaintly ordered,/And better in my mind not under-took' (ll.6–7). However, when Launcelot brings Jessica's note to Lorenzo and is entrusted with a reply, Lorenzo says that he, at least, is provided with a torchbearer. Solanio and Salerio leave to prepare for the masque, and our suspicions are confirmed. Lorenzo tells Gratiano that Jessica plans to disguise herself as a page, and make her escape carrying his torch in the masque. But she is not intending to leave empty-handed. Shylock's coldness and avarice are to be rewarded not only by the loss of his daughter, but also the loss of money. She has stolen from him gold and jewels.

ACT II SCENE v

The dramatic irony of this scene is highly comic. We have just learnt that Jessica has robbed her father, but here Shylock commands his daughter to ensure that his house and possessions are secure! At this point Shylock appears an object of ridicule, a comic butt. Launcelot is leaving him because he is 'famished in his service' (II, ii, 98), but Shylock thinks he has been too generous, and that Launcelot has been able to 'gormandize' (l.3). Shylock, thus mocked by his former servant, falls into the stock comic role of the Jewish miser, and he is uneasy because he has been dreaming of money bags (ll.17–18). Shakespeare even seems to hint at the grotesque superstition that Jews eat human flesh: Shylock reluctantly decides to accept Bassanio's invitation to dinner in order to 'feed upon/The prodigal Christian' (ll.14–15).

There is perhaps an element of truth in his observation that he is not 'bid for love' (l.13), but our perspective on Shylock in this scene is consistently comic and scornful. Launcelot tells him that there will be a masque that evening, which increases his anxiety that his house should be well protected in his absence. He despises all the qualities of warmth and festivity which we admire in Bassanio and his friends. He wants to lock out all sounds of frivolity, and here we may compare him with Antonio, whose 'purse', 'person' and 'extremist means/Lie all unlocked' (I, i, 138–9). Shylock is mean, mechanical and austere; the Christians, as represented by Antonio, are generous, impulsive and wayward. Note also how Shylock's restrictive tendency is carried even into his speech, where he half speaks in metaphor, 'But stop my house's ears, I mean my casements', before checking himself, and his language, abruptly (l.33; see also I, iii, 22–3). His mind is doggedly literal. Every word characterizes him as an alien amidst the gaiety and colour of Venice. It is also significant that he cannot bear the sound of music (l.29), which is associated above all with the romance and enchantment of Belmont.

It has been argued that Shylock's tragic potential is increased by a genuine affection for his daughter, but the text seems to provide little evidence to support this view. He calls her 'Jessica my girl' (l.15), but appears to value her only as the custodian of his property while he is away. Indeed, he seems to mistrust her even in this role; his suggestion that he may return immediately (l.50) is perhaps a warning to ensure she obeys his instructions. He hints at a latent affection for Launcelot: 'The patch is kind enough' (l.44), but stifles it immediately with remarks about his laziness. Shakespeare takes pains to preclude our sympathy here.

ACT II SCENE vi

Gratiano, Salerio and the other masquers are waiting outside Shylock's house for Lorenzo, who has arranged to meet them there. They are surprised that he has not yet arrived, because lovers are usually early for their engagements. Salerio, with a typically elegant classical allusion, draws a distinction between the enthusiasm of young love and the comparative drudgery of fidelity in marriage (ll.5–7). It is another reminder of the more complex and demanding world which exists outside the rarified atmosphere of the romantic attachments of the play. Gratiano develops the point in a series of analogies comparing the delights of anticipation and novelty with the indifference and disillusionment of experience and habit. Aptly, he concludes with a description of a ship gaily setting off on a voyage, and eventually returning home worn and weather-beaten (ll.14–19). This is an uncomfortably suggestive image. We are reminded of Antonio's argosies, and the dangers of sea and tempest: of those elements which threaten the festive security of the comic world. Moreover, the ship is compared to a 'prodigal' (l.14), which recalls the spendthrift Bassanio. The prodigal leaves home full of hope, but returns in tatters, humbled by his adventures. The transience of human hopes and vitality is powerfully conveyed.

It is only with difficulty that the romantic ideals of the play are preserved from these suggestions of disillusionment. So in this scene, our enjoyment at seeing the old miser confounded by the young lovers only just overcomes the qualms which a detached moral assessment of their actions would bring. The colourful verbal play of Lorenzo and Jessica establishes a tone of fun and relish which seems to be above criticism, but we are nonetheless taken aback by the implications of Gratiano's words. When Jessica says that she will join them as soon as she has stolen more of her father's money, he exclaims: 'Now by my hood, a gentle and no Jew!' (l.51). 'Gentle' is a pun on 'Gentile', and we are inevitably reminded of the fact that Jessica has just broken two of the Ten Commandments: to honour one's parents, and not to steal. She may have proved herself 'true' to Lorenzo, but she is hardly beyond reproach. Only the comic context, the love between Lorenzo and Jessica, and the inability of Shylock to command enough of our sympathy, save her from condemnation.

As they leave, Antonio enters and detains Gratiano. The masque must be cancelled, he says, for the wind has changed direction and Bassanio has decided to set sail at once. Gratiano is quite happy to be away.

ACT II SCENE vii

The scene switches to Belmont for the first of the important scenes concerning the choice of caskets. Each casket has an inscription. The gold one bears the words, 'Who chooseth me shall gain what many men desire'; the silver, 'Who chooseth me shall get as much as he deserves'; and the lead, 'Who chooseth me must give and hazard all he hath' (ll.4–9). This last casket Morocco immediately dismisses as being unworthy of him: 'A golden mind stoops not to shows of dross' (l.20). His egoistical sense of his own worth is stressed as he contemplates the inscription on the silver casket. He has little doubt of it.

His arrogance and self-dependence are significant, since the play stresses the need for friendship, and celebrates the healthy inter-dependence of the other characters (with the obvious exception of Shylock). It is these social qualities which are rewarded in the play.

Moving on to the gold casket, Morocco is sure that the inscription must refer to Portia herself: she is 'what many men desire'. They cross the tumultuous sea as if it were a brook to catch a glimpse of her (ll.44–7). The image is appropriate: in Belmont, the threatening external forces symbolized by the sea are soothed and obliterated by the enchantment of romance.

The correct casket contains Portia's portrait, and Morocco decides that only a gold casket would be the appropriate container. It is ironic that he asked Portia not to judge him by his external appearance, but makes the same mistake himself.

His choice is thus highly symbolic. Inside the casket he finds a death's-head and a lyric taunting his mistake. Mortality and failure are the reward of those who judge by outside appearances, and who are more bold than wise. But even Belmont is not entirely free from the play's disturbing ambiguities. The artificial, romance world has been used to make a clear moral point, but as Morocco leaves, Portia remarks, 'Let all of his complexion choose me so' (l.79). Is she not also judging by external appearances? Her integrity is maintained only because 'complexion' can refer to someone's temperament as well as the colour of their skin, but even in Belmont, it seems, simple moral clarity, established in the contrasts drawn between different characters, is a fragile and vulnerable thing.

ACT II SCENE viii

In Venice, Salerio and Solanio describe Shylock's reaction upon discovering that Jessica has eloped with Lorenzo and a good deal of stolen money. The tone is one of scornful amusement. Shylock cannot decide whether to lament the loss of his daughter or the loss of his money, and as a result his words, as reported by Solanio, become comically confused (ll.15–16). He makes Shylock appear so ridiculous that pity for him is inappropriate, although the description of Shylock's passion being mocked by 'all the boys in Venice' (l.23) may provoke some sympathy.

Solanio provides another sobering thought. Shylock will certainly take his revenge on Antonio if he fails to repay the loan on time. Salerio increases the anxiety by saying that he has heard that a richly laden vessel from their country has been wrecked in the English Channel. They hope it is not one of Antonio's.

The scene ends with Salerio eulogizing Antonio: 'A kinder gentleman treads not the earth' (l.35). Salerio movingly describes Antonio's parting with Bassanio, and stresses his selflessness and the strength of his love. For Antonio, friendship makes life worth living. His affection for Bassanio is indeed great: 'I think he only loves the world for him.' Solanio and Salerio then depart to visit Antonio, to try to raise his spirits.

ACT II SCENE ix

This scene returns us to the wooing of Portia by yet another high-born suitor, the Prince of Arragon, through whom we are given a clear explanation (ll.18–51) of the casket motif. Arragon swears to abide by the terms of Portia's father's will, including the obvious condition that he will never reveal which casket he has chosen. Like Morocco, he wastes little time on the ugly lead casket, but ironically also dismisses the gold on the grounds that the 'fool multitude' (l.25) judge by the outward view without seeing beneath. However, he himself is blinded by the sense of his own importance and merit, and arrogantly decides to 'assume desert' (l.50), and choose the silver casket. When it is opened to reveal a fool's head, it is all that his pride and vanity deserve. The lyric characterizes his egotism as a shadow without real substance: his superficial nobility and wisdom thinly disguise his folly.

When Arragon has left, a messenger enters and announces that a young Venetian is at the gate with news that his lord will soon arrive. The young man's courtesy and the valuable gifts he brings create a very favourable impression. The rich, poetic language of the messenger's speech anticipates the blissful harmony of Bassanio's success in Act III Scene ii. Portia mocks his enthusiasm, but is obviously very anxious to judge for herself (ll.95–9). The audience's keen sense of anticipation is heightened by our knowledge that Nerissa's wish that the new suitor will be Bassanio is sure to be fulfilled

ACT III SCENE i

In Venice, the romantic mood of Belmont is cast aside as Solanio reluctantly confirms the rumours that the sinister forces of the sea have claimed one of Antonio's ships (ll.15–16). Our fears for Antonio's wellbeing are underlined as Shylock enters, enraged by what has happened to him. As usual, Shylock is the butt of Salerio's and Solanio's scorn; again he is characterized as a devil (ll.18–19) and they tease him mercilessly about the loss of Jessica. When he says that his daughter is his own 'flesh and blood' (l.32), Salerio echoes Jessica's conviction that she and her father really have very little in common: 'There is more difference between thy flesh and hers than between jet and ivory' (l.33–4).

Mention of the word 'flesh' is an ominous reminder of the bond between Shylock and Antonio, and Shylock soon brings his tormentors down to earth. Salerio asks what possible good it could do him to claim the forfeit, and Shylock, metaphorically hinting that Jews really do eat human flesh, says that it will 'feed' his revenge (l.49). His famous speech of self-justification follows. He lists the wrongs done to him by Antonio, and all because he is a Jew. Shakespeare has taken pains to provide his audience with sufficient reasons for disliking Shylock as an individual, and Shylock is hardly an unbiased observer, so the audience is unlikely to accept what he says at face value. But this reminder of the depth of Antonio's hatred, which perhaps cannot be explained in purely rational terms, is rather uncomfortable.

Shylock subtly exploits the audience's awareness of the imperfections of the other characters. He says that in taking his revenge, he will only be following the example set by the Christians (ll.62–5). He is as human as they, with 'hands, organs, dimensions, senses, affections, passions' (ll.54–5), and he argues that there is no significant difference between his temperament and motivation and their own.

However, a careful reading of this speech tends to demolish any sympathy we have for Shylock, the scapegoat. In emphasizing his similarity to the Christians, Shylock claims equality only at the lowest levels of human nature, those of pure instinct and the desire for revenge. Antonio, Bassanio and Portia attempt to conform to a more elevated and noble conception of humanity: that of generosity, love and mercy. They may fall short of the ideal, but they do have some success. And we must remember that Shylock's intention here is not to ask for sympathy and understanding, but merely to justify a particularly vicious form of revenge. Once again, the ideals of the play may appear rather flattened, but they are not destroyed.

Tubal, another Jew, enters as Solanio and Salerio are called away to speak to Antonio. He tells Shylock that his daughter cannot be found (ll.74–5), and Shylock's reaction to this destroys any pity we might have for him. It is both comically inappropriate and grotesquely vindictive: he wishes Jessica were dead at his feet with his stolen ducats in her coffin. Note, too, how our contempt is directed at Shylock as an individual, not as a Jew. He says that he has never felt the curse on the Jewish race until now: he is only concerned about himself. His utter selfishness and egotism characterize him as an outsider even amongst his own race. There is no suggestion of a common grievance: he feels that there are 'no sighs but o'my breathing, no tears but o'my shedding' (ll.87–8).

The final exchange between Tubal and Shylock re-establishes our comic perspective. Shylock's grotesque eagerness and delight at the news of Antonio's possible ruin compete with his despair at the news that Jessica has wasted her stolen money. His conflicting emotions give his responses the jerky reflexes of a puppet. The comic effect created combines with further evidence of his vindictiveness to deny our sympathy, although once again there is a potentially tragic appeal in his sorrow at the loss of a particular ring (ll.106–9). For once he seems to value something for its sentimental, rather than financial, value. Thus the complexity of Shylock's character is well illustrated in this important scene.

ACT III SCENE ii

Bassanio is now at Belmont, and he and Portia are obviously already deeply attached to one another. Although she says that it is not love that makes her want him to stay, the strength of her feelings is clear (ll.16–17):

> *One half of me is yours, the other half yours,*
> *Mine own I would say;*

The conflicting demands of showing modesty and the exuberance of love are very becoming, and typical of the appeal of Shakespeare's comic heroines. As if in confirmation of the magical atmosphere of Belmont, Portia overcomes her doubts about the wisdom of the test of the caskets: 'If you do love me, you will find me out' (l.41). The romantic tone is enhanced by music as Bassanio makes his choice. It has been suggested that the song which accompanies Bassanio's speech tells him which casket to choose, since it deals with the inadequacy of an attachment 'engendered in the eyes' (l.67); that is, a love based on external appearances. In addition, the song rhymes on the word 'lead'. However, such clues seem very obscure, and Portia has promised not to cheat (ll.10–12). Moreover, Bassanio would hardly have deliberated for so long had he believed that he had been given the answer in the song.

Bassanio is, at any rate, well aware that a beautiful face may be deceptive: ornament is 'The seeming truth which cunning times put on/To entrap the wisest' (ll.100–101). We remember that he was not taken in by Shylock's pretence of 'kindness'. He therefore rejects the superficial brilliance of gold, and passes quickly over the casket made of silver, which is a symbol of money, trade and commerce, a 'pale and common drudge/'Tween man and man' (ll.103–4). That he chooses the lead casket in preference to the gold suggests the contemporary belief in an ideal love which spurns superficial appearances for the true worth lying hidden beneath. Bassanio's rejection of the silver casket also symbolizes the victory of social and emotional considerations over those dictated purely by money and accounts.

So when Portia describes her 'ecstasy' as an 'excess' (l.112), which is another word for interest or usury, we are encouraged to contrast the warmth and emotion of affairs of the heart with the cold, profit-motivated attitudes of business. But although the frequent use of a commercial language to express love throughout this scene emphasizes this contrast, it may also remind us that even peaceful and distant Belmont is implicated in the rather disturbing business deal struck in Venice.

Bassanio, after all, has financed his expedition with funds provided by Shylock and hopes to become a rich man. Moreover, he chooses the casket with the inscription 'Who chooseth me must give and hazard all he hath', and we admire the reasons for his choice, but the financial and personal 'hazard' is really to Antonio, not Bassanio. However, we are barely aware of these ironies, and they are quelled in the tone of joyful release and generous warmth conveyed in Bassanio's and Portia's professions of love.

For Portia, as for Antonio, money should be used in the service of love: it is only for Bassanio's sake that she wishes she were not only 'A thousand times more fair', but also 'ten thousand times more rich' (l.154). She gives him everything she has, including a ring to symbolize the bond between them, but if he ever parts with it, she says, it will foreshadow the end of their love (ll.172–4).

This happy scene is neatly rounded off when Gratiano and Nerissa announce their intention to be married. You should notice the extent of the characters' dependence on one another. Bassanio's joy is made possible by Antonio. Gratiano's marriage is likewise dependent on Bassanio, for Nerissa would only marry him if Bassanio were to win the hand of her mistress (ll.206–8).

However, a serious intrusion into the romantic atmosphere of Belmont is imminent. Salerio enters with Lorenzo and Jessica, whom he has met on the way. He brings a letter which informs Bassanio that every one of Antonio's ships has been lost to the 'merchant-marring rocks' (l.271). Bassanio explains everything to Portia. In her generosity, she cannot immediately see any difficulty. She declares her readiness to pay the debt many times over, although Jessica has heard Shylock say that he would rather have Antonio's flesh than twenty times the amount (ll.284–8). It says much for Shylock's vindictiveness that his desire for revenge should thus outweigh his avarice. Portia's joyful recognition of the pleasure of giving for love (ll.312–13) and her anxiety that Bassanio should go to his friend's aid as soon as they are married affirm the value of generosity and friendship which Shylock seems bent on destroying.

ACT III SCENE iii

Antonio is placed under arrest, but persuades his gaoler to accompany him to see Shylock in an attempt to reason with him. Shylock behaves like an automaton, mechanically repeating 'I'll have my bond'. He will not listen to a word, saying that Antonio has treated him like a dog, and therefore it is his own fault that he is about to be bitten – 'But since I am a dog, beware my fangs' (l.7). Solanio is quite incapable of seeing the partial justice of the remark, calling him an 'impenetrable cur' (l.18). Antonio realizes that it is useless to appeal to him. Shylock is an outsider and quite heartless.

Antonio's explanation of Shylock's passionate desire for revenge heightens our sympathy and respect for the merchant. In the past, he has saved many debtors from ruin at the hands of Shylock (ll.21–4). His words compare once again Antonio's kindness and generosity with Shylock's greed and spite. Solanio tries to comfort him by saying that the Duke will not enforce the terms of the bond, but Antonio knows that the law must be seen to be upheld. All he desires is that Bassanio should be with him at the end.

ACT III SCENE iv

Lorenzo tells Portia that Antonio is worthy indeed of her generosity. She is quite ready to believe it, for friends often resemble each other, and if Antonio is at all like Bassanio, the money she has spent is a small price to pay in order to save him. Her own modesty cuts her short: 'This comes too near the praising of myself' (l.22).

She asks Lorenzo to take control of the running of her house-hold, saying that she intends to await her husband's return in prayer and contemplation in a monastery. But this is a pretence: she is far too energetic a character to embrace such a passive role. When Lorenzo and Jessica have left, we discover that Portia and Nerissa intend to join Bassanio in Venice in the guise of young men. A servant is dispatched with a letter to Portia's cousin, Doctor Bellario, who will supply the 'notes and garments' (l.51) needed for their voyage. Portia's intentions are not yet clear, but what strikes us most at this point is the relish with which she anticipates playing the part of a 'fine bragging youth' (l.69). She has the temperament of an actress.

ACT III SCENE v

The final scene in the Act consists of comic exchanges between Launcelot, Lorenzo and Jessica, who have remained in Belmont. Its purpose is to mark the passage of time, and to provide light relief before the tension of Antonio's trial. But as in Act II Scene ii, 'pure' comedy is mixed with some of the more serious themes of the play. Our ambiguous response to many of the characters is suggested when Launcelot teases Jessica that she is 'damned' (l.5), and we remember our mixed feelings when she deserted her father and stole his money. Jessica's eloquent praise of Portia (ll.68–77) is a fitting conclusion to the Act. However, the banter continues, and though Lorenzo seems to grow weary of Launcelot's dogged witticisms (ll.40–43), he cannot resist making a few of his own.

ACT IV SCENE i

The lengthy scene containing Antonio's trial is of great importance because it brings together all the main characters for the first time. The concepts of justice and the law are scrutinized closely, and in the process Shakespeare celebrates the qualities of mercy, friendship and love. Shylock is finally defeated, and thus the immediate threat to the golden world of comedy and romance is removed. Yet we are still left with the ambiguities and imperfections of the remaining characters. Shylock has been condemned, but his judges are themselves less than perfect (see pp. 80–82).

The Duke, who presides over the court, is very sympathetic to Antonio. He describes Shylock as 'a stony adversary' (1.4), associating him with the cold, immovable rocks which have wrecked Antonio's ships. The difference between Antonio and Shylock is very marked at this point: Antonio's fiery hatred of Shylock, so vividly described in Act I Scene iii, has abated: 'I do oppose/My patience to his fury ...' (ll.10–11).

Shylock is summoned and the Duke appeals again to 'human gentleness and love' (1.25), but in vain. If the audience is to accept the moral distinctions drawn in this scene between the humanity and mercy displayed by the Christians, and Shylock's vindictiveness, it is vital that Shylock should not elicit our sympathy. So, in explaining his loathing for Antonio, he makes no attempt to justify himself in rational terms, and appeals only to the lowest form of instinct and caprice in man: 'say it is my humour' (1.43). Here Shylock embodies the worst in human nature, providing some justification for Gratiano's accusation later on in the scene that he is the spirit of a wolf in the body of a man (ll.133–8). He believes that someone cannot really hate something that he would not kill (1.67). Antonio realizes that argument is pointless, and wishes only to be done with the business. In his speech (ll.70–83) he describes Shylock's temperament with analogies of the sea, the winds and the wolf, all images of the destructive forces which have throughout threatened the play's comic and romantic mood. It is useless to appeal to Shylock on the grounds of common decency and kindness, since he is so vitally different in every respect from all the other characters. His evil makes clear his role as an outsider.

Shylock firmly believes that he is doing nothing wrong in exacting his revenge. He cannot conceive of a form of justice which transcends an automatic adherence to laws (l.89). He believes that the law should neither be governed by the heart, nor be mitigated with kindness and mercy. He believes that it should be quite ruthless.

But, once more, the audience cannot unreservedly condemn Shylock, or share the exaltation of his rivals. Shylock points out that Christians have many slaves, and treat them badly simply because they own them. Under the same laws of ownership a pound of Antonio's flesh is Shylock's property, to be disposed of as he pleases (ll.90–100). Shylock thus appears a cruel ironist. He plays on the fact that many of the more unpleasant and grotesque aspects of his character, which seem to alienate him so from his environment, are to some extent present in the characters of the Christians. Considered an outsider, with nothing in common with the world in which he moves, Shylock seems merely cruel and vindictive, posing a physical threat to Antonio. But because we are aware of the common failings in Shylock, the Jew, and the Christians, we are also aware of a threat which only just fails to destroy the entire moral structure of the play (see pp. 80–82).

Here, significantly, no one attempts to answer Shylock's accusations. He is insisting that the law be recognized, for without the law society could not survive. At this point, the Duke says that he can halt proceedings if Bellario, a learned doctor of law, does not arrive to give his opinion (ll.104–7). Bellario, we know, is the cousin to whom Portia had sent a messenger on preparing to leave for Venice. Nerissa enters, dressed as a lawyer's clerk, and we soon realize the full audacity of Portia's plan. Nerissa gives the Duke a letter from Bellario, and as Shylock ominously begins to sharpen his knife, we learn its contents. Bellario writes that he is too ill to attend the court in person; instead, he has sent a young lawyer whom he has advised on the case (ll.150–63).

We can scarcely be surprised that this young doctor of law turns out to be Portia in disguise. The situation, is, of course, extremely contrived, and not merely because no one, including her own husband, suspects Portia's true identity. The timing of her entry, the outrageousness of the final judgement against Shylock, the very fact that she knew in advance that the Duke would seek her cousin's advice – all these suggest that some of the magic of Belmont has been carried to Venice. It is as if Shakespeare were deliberately drawing our attention to the fact that happy endings only come about, and the morals which are drawn from them only survive the complexities and ambiguities of life, through the enchanted intervention of outside forces.

Portia introduces poetry, grace and mercy into the harsh realities of the courtroom. When she says that Shylock must be merciful, his mind is still fixed on the dictates of the law, but Portia is not referring to that sort of compulsion. 'The quality of mercy is not strained' (l.181), it is divine, and falls like 'gentle rain from heaven' (l.182). In mankind, it comes from the heart (l.192), and surpasses routine justice and power. In showing mercy, men are most like God. This famous speech stresses the play's main theme: to give freely without hope of profit, as mercy is given, is a blessing both for 'him that gives and him that takes' (l.184). We remember Antonio's generosity, born out of love for Bassanio, for which he is ultimately rewarded, and compare it with Shylock's usury, motivated by avarice and the lust for revenge.

Needless to say, Shylock is not impressed by Portia's eloquence. Still he insists that the law must be applied. It is important to note that Portia gives Shylock every opportunity to relent, and also that Shylock is seen to prepare the way for his own ruin, as if he were digging his own grave. He practically invites divine retribution: 'My deeds upon my head!' (l.203), and increases his comic discomfort by praising Portia's wisdom when she says that nothing can change an established law (ll.215–16). So literal and mechanical are his ways of thought and speech in this scene that they only heighten the comic effect of his downfall. He insists that the terms of his agreement with Antonio be carried out to the letter. The flesh must be cut from the point nearest Antonio's heart, because 'those are the very words' (l.251). When Portia asks Shylock to authorize a surgeon to stand by to stop his victim bleeding to death, he refuses because ''tis not in the bond' (l.259). So he establishes and validates the grounds on which he is finally confounded. Portia can also be a literalist. 'The words expressly are "a pound of flesh"' (l.304); there is no mention of any blood, and if Shylock spills but a drop of Antonio's blood, all his property will be confiscated by the state.

This is a very contrived legal trick, but it is not without a certain poetic justice. Any potential sympathy for Shylock as the victim of a technical quibble is undermined by our amusement at seeing him so carefully prepare the ground for his own destruction. The comic symmetry is almost perfect. Now it is Portia's turn to insist that the law take its course. Realizing his difficult position, Shylock is now prepared to settle for the money, but 'He hath refused it in the open court' (l.335) and may only have 'justice and his bond' (l.336). Not only does he seem to have given Portia the means of thwarting him, he also furnishes his enemies with the very taunts with which they tease him. Gratiano triumphantly echoes the words with which Shylock praises Portia: she is 'an upright judge' (l.320), 'A second Daniel' (l.330). The extreme theatricality of the scene is further emphasized by the way Portia increases the suspense by delaying her judgement until the very last moment. In addition, Shakespeare makes great play of the disguises that Portia and Nerissa adopt, and to some comic effect as both Bassanio and Gratiano declare their willingness to sacrifice their wives to save their friend (ll.279–89).

In this artificial world, problems are solved and a moral code established. But because the solutions seem so contrived we are reminded that things are not quite so simple in real life. Moreover, as we have seen throughout *The Merchant of Venice*, complications arise even in well-heeled society, even in comic situations. This scene is no exception. Undoubtedly, Shylock gets his just deserts, but even as his sentence is debated and pronounced, our admiration for his judges is qualified.

Nonetheless, there are good reasons for praising the conduct of Portia, Antonio and the Duke, and it is perhaps best to concentrate first on the favourable contrast between their behaviour and Shylock's. Portia's knowledge of the laws of Venice has put Shylock completely at their mercy. In seeking to claim payment on the agreement with Antonio, Shylock becomes guilty of intended murder. The penalty is that half of his wealth shall be confiscated by the state, the other half be given to Antonio, and the Duke will control Shylock's destiny. Portia has celebrated the quality of mercy, and the Duke, immediately extending it to Shylock, spares his life (ll.365–6), thereby illustrating 'the difference of our spirit'. In addition, he says that if Shylock shows humility, the state may renounce its claim to half of his property and simply fine him (ll.368–9).

Portia now turns to Antonio, asking him what mercy he can show. He also seems to rise to the occasion. The opening lines of his speech (ll.377–9) are rather ambiguous but seem to suggest that the state should forgo even the reduced penalty of a fine. He says that he will keep the other half, not for himself, but in trust for Jessica; a generous act, since he himself is now very short of money.

However, although Shylock receives clemency at the hands of the court, he still pays a high price in other respects. The conditions of his release are that he must become a Christian, and when he dies all his wealth must go to Lorenzo and Jessica. It is not difficult to imagine the pain and humiliation that a man with such deep antipathy to Christianity must feel. Shylock must also be tormented by the thought that the man who stole his daughter should become his legitimate son and heir. We know exactly what he thinks of 'Christian husbands' (ll.292–4). In the light of the declarations in court by Bassanio and Gratiano that their wives should die in Antonio's place, his views are not without substance.

Portia's manner in confounding Shylock also strikes a discordant note on occasions. She has said that mercy drops from heaven, but she makes Shylock beg for it on bended knees (l.360). Moreover, she seems anxious that he should not be let off completely: when the Duke suggests imposing only a fine, she quickly interjects, 'Ay, for the state, not for Antonio' (l.370). Her tone also changes rather dramatically to suit the occasion: her language is poetic in her speech about the importance of showing mercy, but becomes almost sneering when Shylock is finally beaten – 'Art thou contented, Jew? What dost thou say?' (l.390). We are given an uneasy reminder of Portia's own belief that it is easier to invent moral codes than to practise them (I, ii, 12–17).

Shylock seems devastated, answering only 'I am content' (l.391), and asking permission to leave the court, saying that he is ill. At the end of the scene, our reservations at the treatment of Shylock by his adversaries are tempered by the relief of the other characters at the outcome of the trial, and by our enjoyment of the comic confusion over Portia's identity. In his gratitude (and his continuing ignorance as to the true identity of the unknown lawyer), Bassanio wants to give Portia the three thousand ducats intended for Shylock, which is, of course, her own money. She says that Antonio's freedom is sufficient reward, but when he insists that she accept some token, she selects the ring with which she had made Bassanio promise never to part. At first he refuses, but when Antonio himself insists on her behalf, Bassanio sends Gratiano after her with the ring. Again, it is only the contrived devices of comedy which preserve the characters from heartbreak and condemnation: Bassanio is unaware to whom he has given the ring. This amusing joke is a model for the movement of the play, and especially of this highly complex scene. It is the exaggerated freedom and benevolent artificiality of the comic world which saves Antonio, baffles Shylock, and enables the audience to dismiss its misgivings with laughter. Comedy ultimately triumphs over the darker, complicated world which threatens it, but we are not allowed to forget how contrived and fragile its victory is.

ACT IV SCENE ii

Portia tells Nerissa to find out where Shylock lives, and obtain his signature on the deed conferring all his wealth on Lorenzo and Jessica when he dies. Gratiano enters with the ring and an invitation to dinner; the former is graciously accepted, but the latter declined, for Portia intends to reach Belmont before her husband, and disguise the fact of her absence. Nerissa whispers to her mistress that she will try to obtain Gratiano's ring, which she had also made him promise to keep for ever (ll.13–14). They both relish the thought of teasing their respective husbands when they return.

ACT V SCENE i

In the final scene the difficulties and machinations of the play are to some extent eased and resolved by poetry, music and romance. The setting is idyllic. The young lovers, Lorenzo and Jessica, are talking in a grove bathed in moonlight in front of Portia's house. Their conversation carries us back to the rich and evocative world of classical mythology, but even in this romantic mood hints of the darker elements of life persist. The myths suggest forsaken love, and, as we return to the present, Lorenzo reminds us that their union had a less than perfect beginning (ll.14–15):

> *In such a night*
> *Did Jessica steal from the wealthy Jew* ...

Jessica teases him by saying that his protestations of love were a pretence; her mood is light-hearted and playful, but echoes the tragic implications of the stories of Troilus and of Dido.

Stephano, one of Portia's servants, announces to Lorenzo and Jessica that his mistress will soon return, maintaining the pretence that she has spent the intervening time at a monastery. Launcelot is not far behind, with the news that Bassanio will also be in Belmont before morning. Lorenzo tells Stephano to warn the household of Jessica's imminent arrival, and to return with music. He describes the beauty of the night sky: each star is like an angel singing. He says that immortal souls can appreciate the music of the spheres; human beings have immortal souls like the 'cherubins', but whilst we are imprisoned by the body – 'this muddy vesture of decay' (l.64) – we cannot hear the celestial music. This idea is emphasized throughout the play. Complete harmony and perfection are not the lot of the ordinary characters, even though they live and move in a privileged world. But Lorenzo also eulogizes over the soothing power of earthly music, and declares that anyone who hates music is not to be trusted. Shylock, who was so anxious to shut the sound of 'the vile squealing of the wry-necked fife' out of his house (I I, v, 29), is thus aptly identified with one who 'is fit for treasons, stratagems, and spoils' (l.85).

Portia, love's queen, is welcomed home with music, but her first words continue the rather pessimistic implications of Lorenzo's speech concerning the limitations of human life. She compares the light of a tiny candle when all around is dark to 'a good deed in a naughty world' (l.91), suggesting that goodness is so rare that even small acts of kindness are very conspicuous. As the strains of the music drift over to them, Portia's reflections illuminate and clarify one of the important themes of the play. She feels that the music sounds more beautiful at night, because 'Nothing is good ... without respect' (l.99). That is, nothing is absolutely good in itself, but only relatively good as it is modified by circumstances. The beauty of the nightingale's song is largely due to the fact that it is heard in the evening, when there are few other sounds to interrupt it. Things are beautiful because they suit their environment, not because there are fixed standards of beauty and perfection (ll.102–8). Such are our own feelings about the play. Portia, Bassanio and the others are not perfect in themselves; nor, it seems, are their moral standards. But because they are in harmony with the predominant mood of generosity and romance in Shakespeare's comedy, we celebrate their good qualities and hide our misgivings. Shylock is an outsider and an intruder, and as such is condemned with an ease which would not be possible in the normal outside world. Thus our feelings of admiration and condemnation are put in perspective because they are both products of defined circumstances, of make-believe. This does not mean that the morality of the play is without value, but Shakespeare warns us to take it with a pinch of salt: it is not absolute.

Lorenzo welcomes Portia, who only just has time, before the arrival of Bassanio, Antonio and Gratiano, to remind everyone not to mention her absence from home. It is a happy reunion. Resuming the role of gracious hostess with consummate ease, she extends a warm welcome to Antonio (ll.139–41). In her flexibility (she plays romantic heroine, hostess or lawyer with equal ease), Portia approaches nearest to the true ideal of the play. She exploits the constructive and enjoyable possibilities of any situation to the full, with the awareness that standards of behaviour and judgement vary with circumstances.

Nerissa, on a more light-hearted level, is following her mistress's example. She has succeeded in obtaining Gratiano's ring in her disguise as a lawyer's clerk, and immediately begins to rebuke him for losing it. Dramatic irony is used to comic effect as she teases him mercilessly, suggesting that he has given the ring to another woman (ll.157–60). Portia soon joins in, playing upon Bassanio's embarrassment and feelings of guilt by swearing that *her* husband would never give up his ring. Bassanio is so horrified that he wonders if it would not be best if he cut off his hand and pretended that his ring had been taken by force! It is significant that although Bassanio has failed Portia and broken his promise, he has done so for the best possible reasons. Portia goes on to say that he would not part with his ring for all the money in the world, intending to increase his discomfort (ll.172–4). But it is probably no less than the truth. He gave away the ring for something greater than wealth, spurred by his gratitude and his generosity of heart. Nevertheless, we may also remember that this is not the first time that Bassanio has been generous with other people's gifts, or loans.

Bassanio swears that he has not given the ring to another woman, but to no avail: Portia and Nerissa are now enjoying themselves. They warn their husbands that if they ever meet the doctor of law and his clerk they will go to bed with them, and be as liberal with their favours as Bassanio and Gratiano were with their rings (ll.223–35). Their mood is frivolous, but their words underline the limitations of simple idealism. It may lead to a conflict of interests; unbridled generosity may amount to infidelity.

Bassanio promises that he will never again break his word, and Antonio once more offers to be bound to secure his pledge. On this occasion, he offers his soul as the forfeit (ll.251–3). It is very appropriate that he should thus enter into a bond which transcends the limitations of society's laws, since the play has so often stressed the fallibility of human beings. Portia returns the ring; Bassanio recognizes it, and with a final gibe that she did in fact sleep with the doctor of law on the previous night, she produces a letter from Bellario which explains the identities of the young lawyer and his clerk. The letter also contains good news for Antonio: three of his ships have miraculously arrived at their destinations (ll.275–7). No explanation is offered; Antonio's material reward for his love and generosity represents the triumph of the artificial world over realism and logic. It remains only for Lorenzo and Jessica to be informed of their good fortune, whereby they stand to inherit Shylock's wealth, and for Gratiano to relish the thought of finally taking his wife to bed.

Characters

SHYLOCK

The presentation of Shylock is so powerful that although he only appears in five scenes (less than any of the other major characters), he has often been considered the focal point of the play. This is all the more remarkable because he is not only so painfully at odds with the dominant festive and romantic spirit of any of Shakespeare's other main comedies, but also with much of *The Merchant of Venice*. Shylock has been variously seen as a ludicrous comic butt and a menacing and inhuman ogre; some critics have even felt that he attains the status of a tragic hero. It is a measure of Shakespeare's achievement that the play allows all these interpretations.

However, although fear and, to some extent, sympathy are important considerations in any response to Shylock's character, it is essential to Shakespeare's purpose that a comic perspective be maintained. Because Shylock more often strikes us as a figure of fun, our misgivings are not allowed to affect the happy, idealized mood which dominates all the scenes at Belmont. Similarly, comedy helps to prevent any compassion we might have for him from obliterating the distinctions made between different attitudes to riches, and the contrast drawn between the currency of love and that of money (see pp. 77–9).

One of the ways in which Shakespeare makes Shylock a figure of fun is by exploiting the comic potential of the traditional stage Jew. An Elizabethan audience would often have seen Jews comically caricatured as greedy misers and money-lenders. The association of Jews with devils was a standing joke, and in Act III Scene i, when Solanio sees Shylock, he says that the devil is coming 'in the likeness of a Jew'. We have already noted, in Act III Scene i, Shylock's remark that Antonio 'will feed my revenge', an extension of the grotesque belief that Jews really did eat human flesh. He wears the traditional garb – a 'Jewish gaberdine' (I, iii, 109) – and has the standard comic obsession of a miser. For instance, he is anxious, in Act II Scene v, because he has been dreaming of money bags. Launcelot Gobbo, the clown, complains that he is 'famished' in Shylock's service, but the latter considers himself to have been excessively generous, for when Launcelot declares his intention to serve Bassanio, Shylock says that he will not be able to 'gormandize' as he has done in the past.

Such a comic appeal to the popular prejudices of the time might have been enough to prevent Shylock from becoming a purely tragic or fearsome figure to a Shakespearean audience, but rather more is needed to satisfy today's audience. Modern sensibilities are more likely to be outraged than amused by such pointedly racist jokes. However, our view of Shylock moves beyond simple racial discrimination: we laugh at the individual, at his speech, mannerisms and behaviour. When we first meet Shylock in Act I Scene iii, his responses have the imitative quality of a well-trained parrot, echoing Bassanio's words ('Three thousand ducats, well ... For three months, well ... Antonio shall become bound, well.') Such repetition, and its comic effect, is a characteristic of Shylock's speech throughout the play. It is noteworthy that Shylock speaks in just such a comically repetitive manner even as we are about to feel sympathy for him after he has been robbed and deserted by his daughter.

Tubal is relating instances of Jessica's extravagance, and tells Shylock that she has swapped a precious ring for a monkey. For a moment Shakespeare seems to suggest that a little compassion is due to Shylock, as he is for once shown to prize something for more than its purely commercial value: 'I had it of Leah when I was a bachelor' (III, i, 111–12). However, our pity turns to amusement when he reiterates the word 'monkey' in a comically inappropriate affirmation of how much he prized the ring – he would not have given it away for 'a wilderness of monkeys'. Repetition of 'monkeys' makes it seem that 'a wilderness of monkeys' is the most valuable thing which he can think of. It is a masterful example of comic anti-climax, or bathos. Note, too, that Shylock appears ridiculous even in conversation with one of his own people, which illustrates the point that we are laughing at the individual rather than the race. Tubal, a minor character, comes out of it relatively untouched.

We see similar verbal dithering from Shylock a little earlier in this episode. Shylock's reaction to his plight, as reported by Solanio, has already brought a note of scornful amusement into the proceedings. Shylock's mind is so torn between lamenting the loss of his money and the loss of his daughter that his verbal association becomes comically confused (II, viii, 15–16):

> *My daughter! O my ducats! O my daughter!*
> *Fled with a Christian! O my Christian ducats!*

Solanio's account, though undeniably funny, does not necessarily condemn Shylock in our eyes, partly because we know that Solanio is not above a little Jew-baiting, and partly because it is to Shylock's credit that his first exclamation concerns his daughter rather than his money. We may even pity Shylock when we hear that all the boys in Venice are following him and mocking his affliction. However, if we are prepared to be sympathetic when we see his passion and confusion for ourselves, we are to be let down badly. Once again, Shakespeare temporarily draws out our compassion ('My own flesh and blood to rebel!' (III, i, 31) and then erases it: 'I would my daughter were dead at my foot, and the jewels in her ear!' (III, i, 80–81). It is another comic anticlimax, in which a potentially tragic moment degenerates into mere farce because of an inappropriate response.

Shylock's love of money thus destroys any natural human feelings. But just as Shakespeare's appeal to the audience's sense of the ridiculous is focused on an individual rather than a race, so Shylock's very miserliness is so much a part of his individual character that we are not really justified in considering him to be typical of his race. Indeed, his egotism is so great that his feeling for his own people is defined in purely personal terms. Although he partly justifies his desire for revenge by pointing out that Antonio dislikes Jews, he seems incapable of appreciating the prejudices that Jews have suffered with any intensity, until his money is stolen. Instinctively he declares that his experience is the first genuine example of the sufferings of the Jews: 'A diamond gone cost me two thousand ducats in Frankfurt! The curse never fell upon our nation till now' (III, i, 76–8); only then does he correct himself: 'I never felt it till now.' Therefore, ironically, the depth of Shylock's passion for money isolates him even from his own race. His forbears' sufferings have not succeeded in making him feel the curse; only personal financial loss can bring it home to him. So, just as we laugh at Shylock (but not Tubal) a little later in the scene, here our contempt is emphatically focused on the individual. It is also worth noting how Shylock's denial of any brotherhood of spirit with his own race undermines the authoritative tone of his speech in his frequent references to the great and ancient names from Scripture. Moreover, such references to august names are usually used to lend weight in conversations justifying his own sharp practices.

Shylock, then, is an outsider not only because he is a Jew, but because of his selfishness and the way he talks and behaves. During our reading of the play, we realize that the fact that he is a Jew is only one of the many things which separate and alienate him from the prevailing mood and atmosphere. His isolation is at least partly of his own choosing, and he outrages the gregariousness, or social and community spirit, of his environment. His entry in Act I Scene iii puts a stop to the colourful, playful and gracious talk which we have enjoyed in the first scene. His is the language of the hard businessman, and contains no touches of warmth or levity. The Duke calls him, with justification, a 'stony adversary' (IV, i, 4) because he is not only stubborn but cold. He is extremely reluctant to feast with Bassanio (though there is much truth in his observation, 'I am not bid for love, they flatter me' (II, v, 13). He is also peevishly insistent that his house is properly secured in his absence, not merely to protect his property, but because he is worried that his 'sober house' (II, v, 35) will be tainted with the sounds of the celebrations taking place outside.

Shylock despises all frivolity and festivity. He has no sense of humour whatsoever. It is therefore ominous that he should pretend that the terms of the bond by which he puts Antonio at his mercy are a game, a joke: he calls it 'merry sport', a 'merry bond'. The audience is well aware that this is pure hypocrisy, having already heard

Shylock relishing the opportunity to 'feed fat the ancient grudge' (I, iii, 44) he bears Antonio. Even Bassanio is suspicious: 'I like not fair terms, and a villain's mind' (I, iii, 176). His instincts are right. Shylock is at his most sinister when he is pretending to be kind.

We see, too, Shylock the ogre. It could be argued that his determination to have his pound of flesh is fuelled by justifiable anger at the theft of both money and daughter by a Christian, and a friend of Antonio's at that. However, it seems highly unlikely that Shylock would lose the opportunity to take a more conventional form of interest, unless he really intended to enforce the terms of his bond. Moreover, we learn from Antonio (Act II Scene iii) that Shylock has in the past been quite willing to ruin other victims of his usury, and that he probably hates Antonio partly because he has helped just such people.

It is said that Shylock's innate humanity is displayed only towards his daughter. But we have seen how his grief for her loss is overwhelmed by his pain at the loss of his money, and soon turns into vindictiveness. He wants not only to see Antonio dead, but Jessica as well. Nor do we see any genuine signs of affection for her before she deserts him. He calls her 'my girl' (II, v, 15), but shows little tenderness; he seems more concerned about the safety of his property: 'Look to my house ... Lock up my doors ... Do as I bid you; shut doors after you./Fast bind, fast find'.

We are more likely to see the human side of Shylock's character in his famous speech of self-justification (III.1.48–66). He claims that Antonio has insulted and thwarted him for one reason only: that he is a Jew. The audience is likely to see this as over-simplification, having already been presented with far more compelling reasons for disliking Shylock as an individual. But Shylock might have some justification for his observation, for we have no reason for thinking that Antonio is any less anti-semitic than his fellow Venetians. Shylock goes on to point out that a Jew is as human as the next man. Who can deny it? But it is vital to realize that even in this, his most lucid, articulate and incisive speech, Shylock ironically displays something of the inhumanity by which he is himself condemned. As many commentators have pointed out, the speech is not a plea for equality, but a justification for revenge. Of course Jews are human beings, but where is Shylock's own humanity and warmth? He claims equality with the basest level of human nature, the desire for revenge; and much of the rest of the speech emphasizes his similarity to other people simply in terms of flesh and blood. We may reserve our judgement on Gratiano's characterization of Shylock as a wolf in the body of a man (IV, i, 133–8), since he has 'affections, passions', but Shylock displays none of those feelings of love, generosity and warmth which normally raise men above the level of animals. He has eyes, hands, organs, passions; he has blood but, significantly, makes no mention of his heart. In many ways what Shylock says here recalls nothing so much as his use of the word 'good', when he and Bassanio are discussing Antonio in Act I Scene iii. Shylock has no interest in the morality of his fellow humans, but judges them only by his own limited system of values. To be 'good' is to have money; to be human is to seek revenge.

The terms of the bond are thus well chosen, for Shylock wants to strip everything down to the bare bones. He despises or ignores all the trappings of society which transcend the basic mechanisms of life: generosity, elegance, politeness, festivity and poetry. This last, his hatred of figurative language (presumably because of its frivolity), is comically illustrated by his own habits of speech. On two of the rare occasions that he is tempted to toy with metaphor he checks himself abruptly, and explains himself in literal terms: by 'water thieves' (I, iii, 22) he points out, unnecessarily, he means pirates; and 'my house's ears' (II, v, 33) are 'my casements'.

This literal habit of mind reaches a grotesque climax during the trial scene. Shylock insists that the exact words of the bond are fulfilled. The flesh must be cut from Antonio's breast because the document specifies the point ' "Nearest his heart"; those are the very words' (IV, i, 251). Again, when Portia suggests that a surgeon should be at hand to stop Antonio bleeding, Shylock will have none of it because ''tis not in the bond' (IV, i, 259). He relies on the letter of the law and cannot conceive of a form of justice which goes beyond this. He feels, therefore, that he has nothing whatsoever to fear, because he believes he is acting strictly in accordance with the laws of Venice: 'What judgement shall I dread, doing no wrong?' (IV, i, 89). It is therefore most appropriate that he is ultimately condemned by an even more literal interpretation of the terms of the bond than his own. It contains no mention of the word 'blood', so if he spills any his lands and goods will be confiscated. Shylock has dug his own grave, and because the audience perceives him doing this, the play retains its comic perspective to the end.

The Merchant of Venice thus provides ample reasons for considering Shylock to be both a ludicrous and a very menacing figure. The combination of these aspects of his character prevent him from assuming a genuinely tragic stature. However, we cannot get away from the realization that, in spite of our amusement, contempt and fear, a modicum of pity still remains for Shylock.

One of the reasons for this is that Shylock is only carrying to a logical, if determined, extreme things he does not control, that have been created by the world with which he is at such odds. When he insists on his pound of flesh we may be appalled, but we should also be aware that he is only appealing to the laws of property and punishment upon which all society is based. Moreover, although Shylock seems to be so completely out of touch with those around him, there are latent similarities with them. He is devoid of compassion but, despite Portia's eloquent speech on the 'quality of mercy' (I V, i, 181–202), the mercy extended to Shylock is perhaps rather less than the ideal spirit of Christian forgiveness. Similarly, although Antonio particularly despises Shylock's method of money-lending, he is not above borrowing from him when the need arises.

Thus we do begin to sympathize a little with Shylock when we see the flaws in the characters of his adversaries. However ludicrous and evil Shylock may appear, one cannot feel wholly easy about his treatment if one doubts, even for a moment, the integrity of his accusers. Moreover, Shylock is certainly not stupid, and he seizes upon their latent hypocrisy and exploits it to the full. When Antonio is forced, by his own generosity, to ask Shylock for money, Shylock makes the most of his advantage. Antonio has called him a dog and Shylock sarcastically asks (I, iii, 118–19):

> *Hath a dog money? Is it possible*
> *A cur can lend three thousand ducats?*

There is a biting logic in Shylock's passion here, just as in his speech during the trial when he points out that the Christians feel free to treat their slaves as they like because they are their property (IV, i, 90–100). By the same laws, a pound of Antonio's flesh belongs to Shylock, to use as he will. So although Shylock cannot by his personality command our sympathy, we may begin to consider him as something of a scapegoat. He pays the price for his own evilness, but the Christians themselves are far from perfect.

Shakespeare also suggests that the Venetians are partly responsible for creating the monster in their midst. Shylock loathes Antonio with a passion which is reciprocated. He vividly describes his treatment (I, iii, 102–15). He has not only been abused, but spat upon and kicked. The implication is clear: if you kick a dog, you should not be altogether surprised if it tries to bite you. Once again Shylock himself drives the point home (III, iii, 7–8):

> *Thou call'dst me dog before thou hadst a cause,*
> *But since I am a dog, beware my fangs.*

Shylock must remain a comic rather than a tragic figure, but for the first time in the English theatre the Jew has justifiable cause for complaint.

ANTONIO

Antonio plays a surprisingly small role considering the play is named after him. He appears to have very little control over his own fate. His passivity is partly explained by the fact that he is a victim of circumstance: of Shylock's vindictive machinations, and of the destructive, inhuman forces of sea and tempest. But he also seems temperamentally rather listless. In this, his character contrasts with the animation and optimism of Bassanio, Portia and their circle of friends. But he is certainly not an outsider in the way that Shylock is. His warmth and generosity clearly identify him with the ideals of the play, and although even at the end he is, conspicuously, the

only unmarried member of its happy group of celebrants, he nonetheless fits into the magical and romantic environment of Belmont.

Antonio is the model for the benevolence of civilized wealth, showing how money can be used in the name of love, to enable Bassanio
to win his bride. He is open and generous almost to a fault: having
already lent Bassanio large sums to subsidize an extravagant life style,
he unhesitatingly puts himself and his 'extremest means' at his friend's
disposal in his latest venture (I, i, 135–9). In stark contrast to Shylock's
frantic concern for the security of his property, Antonio's purse is
'all unlocked' (I, i, 139). Moreover, Bassanio is not the only one to
have benefited from his kindness and financial support. Shylock hates
him because he always lends money without taking interest (I, iii, 40–
42), and because he has saved many people from complete ruin
(III, iii, 21–4). Antonio condemns usury out of hand; he is a symbol
of the rather idealistic medieval attitude that money should be lent
out of Christian charity, not for personal profit.

This principle is not simply a matter of intellectual conviction; it
has its deepest source in love. Unlike Shylock, who only recognizes
the power of legal contracts, Antonio is compelled by the emotional
bonds of friendship. Bassanio need only say what he should do, and
he is 'prest unto it' (I, i, 160). The strength of his love is vividly conveyed by Salerio, when he describes the two friends' farewell as
Bassanio leaves for Belmont. Antonio is as liberal with his feelings
as he is with his money (II, viii, 46–9):

> And even there, his eye being big with tears,
> Turning his face, he put his hand behind him,
> And with affection wondrous sensible
> He wrung Bassanio's hand ...

This testimony to the tenderness of Antonio's feelings is very touching,
but still more admirable is his utter unselfishness. When Solanio says
that he thinks Antonio 'only loves the world' for his friend (II, viii, 50),
the extent of his self-sacrifice is clear. It is not simply that by accepting
Shylock's bond he has put his life in jeopardy. By giving Bassanio
the means to woo Portia, Antonio inevitably risks his own happiness.
He is prepared to share Bassanio – his very reason for living – with

Portia. Thus Salerio's eulogy seems quite appropriate at this point: 'A kinder gentleman treads not the earth' (I I, viii, 35).

The nobility and sincerity of Antonio's spirit is elegantly framed by his economical, highly polished conversation. His farewell to Solanio and Salerio (I, i, 62–4), for instance, shows enormous social grace. However, although he is not reticent in Bassanio's company, beside the expansiveness and gaiety of his other friends he appears rather subdued. His vague melancholy wearies not only himself, but those around him (I, i, 1–2). At this stage we are unlikely to pay much attention to the rebukes and admonitions of Gratiano, who speaks 'an infinite deal of nothing' (I, i, 114), but as the play progresses, the gloominess of Antonio's character becomes more and more pronounced.

His 'want-wit sadness' (I, i, 6) in the first scene has no immediately obvious source, although it may be explained by his realization that Bassanio wishes to marry, and will perhaps soon be lost to him. When Antonio is furnished with tangible reasons for grief by the wrecking of his ships, the absence of his friend and the vengefulness of Shylock, meditative melancholy becomes almost a death wish (I V, i, 115–16):

> *The weakest kind of fruit*
> *Drops earliest to the ground, and so let me.*

Antonio is undeniably in a desperate plight, but there is more than a suggestion of self-indulgence in his words, almost as if he were morbidly revelling in thoughts of martyrdom. Of course, Antonio has good reason to believe that his plight is hopeless, because Shylock seems quite merciless. But he does not merely accept his fate: he practically welcomes it. In the first scene, Solanio comes to the conclusion that Antonio's misery is due to his being an innately depressed character. When Bassanio has left for Belmont, the young gallant again draws our attention to this rather self-indulgent trait in the merchant's character: Antonio has 'embraced' despair (I I, viii, 53). So, right up to the moment of his reprieve, Antonio extracts every drop of pathos from his predicament. He seems to offer himself as a helpless sacrificial lamb, passively accepting his fate (I V, i, 114–15):

> *I am a tainted wether of the flock,*
> *Meetest for death.*

As he speaks what he believes are his last words, he tells Bassanio
not to grieve, but his speech is hardly calculated to relieve his friend's
intense feelings of pain and guilt. Saying that his life would be so
'wretched' and poor if he were spared, that death is welcome to him,
is not likely to provide much comfort for Bassanio. Antonio's emotive
appeal can only intensify rather than assuage the guilt: 'Say how I
loved you, speak me fair in death' (IV, i. 272).

A picture is thus drawn of a generous and affectionate person,
instinctively unselfish, but touched with a strain of rather self-
indulgent melancholy and even morbidity. Above all, Antonio seems
gentle and passive, opposing 'patience' to Shylock's 'fury' (IV, i, 11).
But there is a hidden irony here. In his earlier dealings with Shylock
he has shown few signs of 'quietness of spirit' (IV, i, 12): indeed, he
has displayed a vehement hatred which seems difficult to reconcile
with our overall impression of his character.

A hint of what is to come in his first meeting with Shylock (Act
I Scene iii) is suggested by the absence of his customary politeness.
It is at once clear that he does not like Shylock, for no greeting is
offered, and Antonio seems to be intentionally rude in talking of
Shylock in the third person as he speaks to Bassanio (I, iii, 60–61). But
this cannot prepare us for the account of Antonio's treatment of
Shylock, which indicates a complex reversal of their relationship in
the trial scene. Shylock has been insulted, spat upon and kicked, and
he has 'borne it with a patient shrug' (I, iii, 106). Antonio indicates that
he would do the same again. We know that he despises usury, but
this is not enough to explain such a violent hatred in a character who
is normally so gentle and passive. Antonio seems to undergo a complete
transformation in his relationship with Shylock. Towards the end of
the scene some attempt is made to play down this rather distasteful
side of his character. When Shylock affects kindness in offering his
'merry bond', Antonio is prepared to take him at his word. Showing
some of the generosity of spirit which he reveals towards the other

characters, he is willing to think the best of Shylock's motives: 'Hie thee, gentle Jew ... he grows kind' (I, iii, 174–5).

However, such brief magnanimity is not enough to shift the disturbing impression that Antonio has descended to Shylock's own low level. Indeed, it seems as if Antonio himself initiated the spite, and is therefore responsible for their mutual degradation. As the play develops, Antonio's moral superiority is re-established and frequently stressed, but this darker side to his nature, though outweighed by his good qualities, is never quite forgotten.

As Lorenzo points out (V, i, 63–5), human beings may not attain perfect harmony, and Antonio reveals that perfection is not possible even for the hero of Shakespearean comedy. This explains the depth of his hatred for Shylock. Antonio is an idealist; he despises anything that reminds him of the harsh and complicated world which intrudes into the play and threatens idealism. Shylock's usury symbolizes this darker environment. But even more galling for Antonio is that he himself cannot avoid usury. He loathes Shylock's business, but is compelled by circumstance to use it. He feels forced to be a hypocrite, and when Shylock revels in his embarrassing position he is so galled that he initiates his own tragedy, telling him to lend the money as he would to an enemy (I, iii, 132–4), with all the consequences.

Antonio's involvement in an imperfect world goes deeper than this. A modern audience at least will find it difficult to swallow the naïve moral distinction between making profits from trade and from usury. Shylock argues that there are many different ways of taking interest, citing the biblical story of how Jacob thrived by his skill in breeding sheep (I, iii, 73–87). He suggests by this that there are no such things as natural and unnatural ways of making money. Antonio tries to counter his argument by saying that Jacob's fortune was the will of God, but his implication that farmers (and merchants) enjoy heaven's blessing, whilst money-lenders are damned, is rather strained. We approve of the generous spirit which lies behind Antonio's convictions, but we cannot completely accept their practical application. Both merchant and money-lender are out to make a profit.

A similar form of qualified sympathy and admiration is evoked in the trial scene. There is no doubt that Antonio extends mercy to Shylock far beyond the demands of the law. However, by his insistence that Shylock must become a Christian, and make a will nominating the man who stole his daughter as his heir, he ensures that he is not allowed to escape all retribution. Moreover, by keeping half of Shylock's wealth in trust for Lorenzo and Jessica, he once again, if indirectly, soils his hands with the profits of usury.

Antonio is, therefore, a failed idealist. In some ways he seems too noble for the world, but he is unable to escape the complexities and ambiguities which persist even in the privileged and rarefied environment of comedy. He is ultimately rewarded for his generosity and love, but his hypocritical tendencies draw attention to the fact that any form of idealism in human beings is fragile, and that moral clarity, even in a comedy, is hard won. Therefore at the end of the play, in guaranteeing Bassanio's pledge never again to break a promise, Antonio aptly enters into a bond which transcends human understanding, and points towards God (V, i, 251–3). This time his soul will be the forfeit.

PORTIA

Portia is a golden prize. She is both exceedingly beautiful and extremely rich; a priceless object of desire (I, i, 169–70):

> *her sunny locks*
> *Hang on her temples like a golden fleece,*

This description of a fair-haired beauty associates Portia with the ideal of the Venetian School of painting, but it is the only detail we have of her physical appearance. It is left to the reader's imagination, or to the discretion of a director, to complete the picture. Shakespeare conveys her beauty by its immense power to attract. 'All the world desires her', and suitors come 'From the four corners of the earth' to pay homage to 'this mortal breathing saint' (II, vii, 38–40). The suggestion of Portia's divinity in Morocco's words emphasizes the goodness which enhances her beauty. Bassanio has also stressed she is not only 'fair', but of 'wondrous virtues' (I, i, 162–3). However, she is no passive paragon of virtue. She displays enormous energy and resilience. In Portia, as in so many of Shakespeare's comic heroines, beauty is animated by a vigorous spirit.

In many ways Portia is the dominant figure in the play, with an authority and control unmatched by any other character. It is not surprising, then, that at first she seems highly dissatisfied with her father's will which deprives her of the power to choose her own husband. However, unlike Antonio, it is not in her nature to indulge in melancholy. She quickly overcomes her weariness in her festive mocking of the many hopefuls who have come to Belmont to try to win her hand. In Portia grace and tact are delightfully set off by a rather mischievous sense of humour. For instance, when Morocco asks her not to judge him by his dark complexion, she subtly replies that he is as handsome a man as any of the suitors she has yet seen (I I, i, 20–22). He is reassured, not understanding the hidden joke: she feels nothing but contempt and revulsion for all of her suitors. But Portia is never allowed to appear merely cynical. She has great optimism and exuberance. When a messenger later announces the arrival of a very striking 'ambassador of love' (I I, ix, 92), she mocks him for his unrestrained enthusiasm. Nonetheless, it is clear that she is really very excited at the prospect of meeting him (I I, ix, 95–9).

This attractive combination of affected detachment and inner zeal is at its most appealing in her speech to Bassanio as he prepares to make his choice of the caskets. Something tells her that she does not want to lose him; her modesty compels her to deny that it is love, but her ardour gives her away (I I I, ii, 1–24). As he proceeds, all vestiges of pretence evaporate in romanticism, love and open admiration (I I I, ii, 53–5):

> *Now he goes,*
> *With no less presence but with much more love*
> *Than young Alcides ...*

The strength of her love matches that of Antonio, but whereas his was conveyed in the parting with his friend by emotional speechlessness, when Bassanio chooses the right casket Portia's love bursts out in a torrent of words (III, ii, 108–14). This contrast in their temperaments is marked; nonetheless, it should be noted that they share many admirable qualities. Antonio put his money and his person at Bassanio's disposal for the sake of love, and Portia matches his generosity in every respect (III, ii, 166–7):

> *Myself and what is mine to you and yours*
> *Is now converted.*

She too values money only in so far as it can be used for the sake of love and friendship: she wishes she were 'ten thousand times more rich' (III, ii, 154) because she wants to be perfect in Bassanio's eyes. So, when she hears of Antonio's distress she immediately offers to pay the debt twenty times over, if necessary, happily seizing the opportunity to use her money in the service of the heart (III, ii, 299–314). She is quite unselfish. Just as Antonio has given Bassanio the means to win Portia without a thought for his own happiness, she provides her husband with the money to reclaim Antonio from Shylock's clutches, urging him to leave as soon as they are married. She selflessly curtails the celebrations of her own wedding day. The symmetry of love and generosity in Antonio and Portia is thus perfect; the happiness of each is dependent on the unselfishness of the other, and meets in Bassanio.

To give for the sake of friendship, without expectation of personal profit – indeed, in a spirit of self-sacrifice – is the Christian ideal. Lorenzo feels that Portia embodies it; she has 'a noble and true conceit/ Of godlike amity' (III, iv, 2–3). This association of the disinterested liberality of friendship with the divine is highlighted by Portia in her famous speech on 'The quality of mercy' (IV, i, 181–99). Mercy epitomizes unselfish generosity, and in displaying it human beings become closer to God (IV, i, 192–4):

> *It is an attribute to God himself,*
> *And earthly power doth then show likest God's*
> *When mercy seasons justice.*

As Lorenzo has said, Portia has a highly developed understanding of the value of Christian fellowship, but it must be remembered that although this qualifies her for her role as judge in this scene, she falls some way short of the perfection of divine forgiveness. She offers Shylock only a beggar's mercy: 'Down ... and beg mercy of the Duke' (IV, i, 360). Moreover, when the Duke is merciful, sparing Shylock's life and suggesting that he may substitute a fine for the half of Shylock's goods which should go to the state, she seems anxious that he should not escape all retribution: 'Ay, for the state, not for Antonio' (IV, i, 370). She even revels in her success, gloating over Shylock's discomfort (IV, i, 390): 'Art thou content, Jew? What dost thou say?'.

Even Portia, whose control over events sometimes seems to border on divine authority, is not perfect. But in realizing this, we appreciate the importance of the difference in temperament between Portia and Antonio. He is dispirited, almost paralysed by the darker elements of life, but she accepts them, and is not downcast. She is well aware of her own shortcomings, and of the fact that imperfection is in the nature of human beings, who are often guided by emotions rather than moral precepts (I, ii, 14–18):

> *It is a good divine that follows his own instructions. I can easier teach twenty what were good to be done than to be one of the twenty to follow mine own teaching. The brain may devise laws for the blood, but a hot temper leaps o'er a cold decree ...*

So, complete harmony may not be found, but Portia does not therefore abandon the struggle. She understands and exalts the value of moral ideals such as mercy, and strives to conform to them, with some success. Her imperfection lies simply in her humanity, and it must be remembered that without this humanity all would be lost. Emotional involvement may prevent Portia from attaining the perfect spirit of forgiveness which she has articulated so well, but without her love for Bassanio and his friend the trial would have a far more unpleasant conclusion. Feelings, imperatives of the 'blood', result in inconsistencies, but in the absence of love a 'cold decree' such as the law of property could be merely destructive. Portia strains for the ideal, trusts to her heart, and is rewarded for it.

She thus makes the best of a world which she acknowledges to be imperfect, and alters her image to suit the demands of each new situation. She can play a child, remote and innocent in an enchanted world, 'an unlessoned girl, unschooled, unpractisèd' (I I I, ii, 159). But she is also a woman of resource and command, a beautiful object of desire, a mischievous schoolgirl, and an authoritative lawyer. Her actress's temperament is ideally suited to the privileges and the freedom of the world of the comic stage: she dons her lawyer's costume and saves the day. Portia is not immune to the imperfections which threaten the golden world in the play, but through her love, her generosity and her sensitivity to her surroundings she orchestrates the triumph of comedy and romance.

BASSANIO

Bassanio is the lucky beneficiary of the wealth and generosity of Antonio and Portia. He has few funds with which to be free, but does not let this interfere with his innate liberality and enjoyment of the good life. He is something of a spendthrift, his carelessness with money being diametrically opposed to the accounting mechanisms of hard business practised by Shylock. He has thus run up large debts, mostly to Antonio, by indulging in a lifestyle way beyond his means (I, i, 122–31). His extravagant optimism is well illustrated by the fact that, realizing he must make some attempt to put his affairs in order, he proposes to solve his financial problems by marrying into money. Rather than curtail his spending, he seeks to dispense with the need for restraint: Portia's money will settle his debts and allow him to be prodigal with impunity. Needless to say, the success of his plan depends on yet another loan. Bassanio's attitude towards money is naïve, but also appealing and, in the context of the play, admirable. He sees it as the servant of social relations, and therefore cannot conceive of any incompatibility between goodness, love and money. Portia is desirable because she is virtuous, beautiful and rich, and we can only warm to Bassanio as he determines to solve his financial problems by winning his heart's desire.

However, although he himself describes his proposals as naïve, they are not really the result of 'pure innocence' (I, i, 145). It may be inappropriate for us to judge by modern standards and to condemn Bassanio as a fortune-hunter, yet, by describing his marital aspirations as 'plots' (I, i, 133) and anticipating the 'thrift' (I, i, 175) which he will incur, he shows that he is not simply an artless romantic. Our admiration of Bassanio, as of Portia and Antonio, is occasionally uneasy.

Nonetheless, the most striking aspects of his character are his warmth and sociability. His first words, greeting Salerio and Solanio, are typical of his gregarious nature (I, i, 66–7):

> *Good signors both, when shall we laugh? Say, when?*
> *You grow exceeding strange. Must it be so?*

Obviously Bassanio's financial difficulties have yet to make any inroads into his social life, for that evening he is holding a feast for all his 'best-esteemed acquaintance' (II, ii, 159). Even when doing business, he uses the vocabulary of friendship and gaiety: 'Will you pleasure me?', he asks Shylock (I, iii, 7), and, unlike Antonio, retains his courteous demeanour in his relations with Shylock, inviting him to dine with them (I, iii, 30).

Bassanio is thus a gentleman in every sense of the word, and in these opening scenes he fully justifies Nerissa's praise that of all the men she has seen he is the 'best deserving a fair lady' (I, ii, 108–10). Like Portia, he understands that standards of conduct and judgement vary with circumstances, warning Gratiano that if he is to accompany him to Belmont, he must moderate his 'wild behaviour' (II, ii, 174). He himself blends perfectly with the atmosphere of enchantment and love in Belmont: as a suitor he is chivalrous and graceful, and his words have the luxuriant lyricism of the ideal romantic hero. More-over, it is clear that beneath the polished exterior of his elegant gallantry runs a strong vein of sincere love and passion (III, ii, 175–6):

> *Madam, you have bereft me of all words.*
> *Only my blood speaks to you in my veins . . .*

Bassanio earns his good fortune; his prosperity symbolizes the victory of human relationships over affairs of money.

But it is not only in his love and gregariousness that he seems to have, as Launcelot says, 'the grace of God' (II, ii, 139–40). He is sensitive and perceptive, and has the ability to see beneath the surface of things, an essential capacity in an imperfect world. So unlike Antonio, he is instinctively suspicious of Shylock's pretence of kindness and generosity in the wording of the bond: 'I like not fair terms and a villain's mind (I, iii, 176). It is exactly this awareness that things may not be as they seem which enables him to win Portia: he rejects the golden casket because 'ornament', a beautiful exterior, may be 'The seeming truth which cunning times put on/To entrap the wisest' (III, ii, 100–101). We know that Bassanio is careless of money, and he passes over the silver, which symbolizes it, with barely a glance. By choosing the lead casket he shows himself as one who scorns to judge by superficial appearances, identifying his love for Portia as something far deeper and more noble than mere physical attraction.

In spite of all this, there is a certain irony in Bassanio's choice. He rejects the lure of money and ornament symbolized by the silver and gold caskets, but he feels that in order to woo Portia he must have sufficient means to enhance and embellish his suit. Moreover, he is impressed by the inscription which threatens rather than promises: 'Who chooseth me must give and hazard all he hath'; but after all it is neither his wealth nor his life which is at stake.

So, although we enjoy and admire Bassanio's carefree liberality, there are times in the play when his purely idealistic and emotional approach might have very unpleasant consequences for those around him. As Antonio stands in peril of his life, Bassanio's extravagant instincts lead him to make an extraordinary declaration: to save his friend, he would sacrifice his own life, all the world, and Portia too (IV, i, 279–84). He may be partially excused such rashness: the offer is made as Bassanio is suffering almost unbearable feelings of pain and guilt. Nevertheless, were it not for the comic appeal of the situation (unbeknown to him, Portia has heard every word), his words would simply shock and outrage.

Here Bassanio is preserved from moral censure because our first instinct is to laugh, and in the play as a whole Shakespeare makes it clear that only the contrivances of comedy prevent his actions from resulting in disaster. It takes all Shakespeare's and Portia's artfulness to save Antonio. Bassanio acts from the best of motives, but, with all the goodwill in the world, difficulties and conflicts of interests arise. For instance, in the ring episode it seems that whatever he does will damage his honour. If he gives it to the 'young doctor', he is being unfaithful; if he keeps it, he could be accused of ingratitude.

Fortunately, comedy licenses extravagance and impulsiveness, and resolves conflict: without knowing it, Bassanio returns the ring to his wife. His fortune is the prodigal's dream come true: the carefree spendthrift is rewarded for his love and liberality, and protected from the complications and dire consequences which might arise in real life, by the devices of an artificial world.

LORENZO

Lorenzo is an elegant, dashing young lover; a carefree knight-errant rescuing his maiden from 'strife' (I I, iii, 20) and a sort of imprisonment in Shylock's austere, secure house, and setting off with her into an unknown future. He typifies the gaiety of the elegant Venetian society in which he moves, light-heartedly teasing his friend Gratiano for his wordiness (I, i, 106–7), and relishing his part in baffling the old miser Shylock. His obvious enjoyment of the romantic, festive mischief of playing the thief for the sake of love dispels our uneasiness at the suggestions of stealth and deceit in the elopement. His sense of fun stresses the pleasure and joy of love, and although he seems to weary of Launcelot's tenacious wit (I I I, v, 40–42) his conversations with Jessica mix lyrical romanticism with playfulness.

Happiness for Lorenzo, as for Bassanio, is dependent on the beneficence of intimate relations. He confides in Gratiano concerning his plans, and their success demands the help of his friends in the masque: it is a conspiracy of friendship and love. It is this appreciation of the value of 'amity' that he so admires in Portia (I I I, iv, 1–4), and his own love and affection earn him his place in Belmont. Indeed, he is perfectly qualified to be the guardian of Portia's home in her absence:

his words at the beginning of the final Act echo her delightful tone of lyricism seasoned with a sense of humour, moving from a rich evocation of mythical love (V, i, 1–6; 9–12) to a rather unromantic description of their elopement (V, i, 14–17).

Their happiness was indeed initiated in less than ideal circumstances of deception and theft, but the quality of Lorenzo's love is greatly to be admired. Like Bassanio's, it looks beneath the surface, perceiving the good qualities which he associates with the Christian religion in the daughter of a Jew: she is 'gentle Jessica' (II, iv, 19), 'gentle' punning on 'gentile'. So, he places her in his 'constant soul' not only because she is 'fair', but also 'wise' and 'true' (II, vi, 56–7). Of course, his celebration of her fidelity has ironic implications: in being constant to Lorenzo, Jessica deserts her father. But just as Portia accepts that imperfection and conflict are inevitable in a 'naughty world', Lorenzo too realizes that perfect concord is not possible on earth while immortal souls are enclosed by the body, 'this muddy vesture of decay' (V, i, 64). He too looks on the bright side, stressing what can be preserved of nobility and goodness. We may be deaf to the choral music of heaven (V, i, 60–65), but earthly music has its own 'sweet power' (V, i, 79) to soothe and ennoble human beings. Anyone who, like Shylock, despises music, 'Is fit for treasons, strategems, and spoils' (V, i, 85). Ironic suggestions persist even here, since Lorenzo won Jessica by a 'strategem', but through his love, optimism and understanding he deserves the indulgence of the comic world and its audience. So riches fall on him like manna from heaven (V, i, 294–5). Because he is one who values love more than money, he is rewarded with both.

JESSICA

Jessica's first speech, like those of Portia and Antonio, conveys a feeling of melancholy. However, she has something of Portia's vitality and sense of humour, liking Launcelot because he is a 'merry devil' (II.3.2) and enjoying playful, teasing conversations with Lorenzo. So she cannot bear the restrictions and tedium of Shylock's sober, austere household. Her resourcefulness and resolve as she disguises herself as a page-boy to escape from home are worthy of Portia herself.

We already know enough about her father to sympathize with her desire to abandon him, and it is clear that the difference in their temperaments makes her present situation intolerable: she has his 'blood', but not his 'manners' (I I, iii, 18–19). Lorenzo and his friends agree. Solanio tells Shylock, 'There is more difference between thy flesh and hers than between jet and ivory' (I I, i, 35–6). She is 'wise, fair, and true' (I I, vi, 56), and her attitude towards money is more in tune with impulsive, careless Christians. On her travels she spends 'Fourscore ducats at a sitting' (I I I, i, 101) and swaps a valuable ring for a monkey, displaying a glorious contempt for material wealth.

Lorenzo is thus justified in describing her love as 'unthrift' (V, i, 16). Like Bassanio, Jessica seems to have a talent for spending other people's money. But whereas Bassanio's liberality is licensed by the love of Antonio, who provides his loans, there is no such sanction for Jessica's extravagance. Stealing is a sin for Christian and Jew alike, as indeed is the failure to honour one's father; our enjoyment of the wasting of Shylock's greedily hoarded wealth is therefore mixed with uncomfortable reflections on Jessica's true integrity. It is to her credit that she understands the moral complications of her position (I I, iii, 16–17):

> *Alack, what heinous sin is it in me*
> *To be ashamed to be my father's child.*

However, she makes no attempt to soften the blow but only aggravates the offence by theft.

Nonetheless, such considerations are not allowed to override our sympathy for her, since her moral difficulties are occasioned by her admirably effusive and loving nature. At any rate we are disarmed by the comic appeal of the elopement, the 'pretty follies' (I I, vi, 37) of young lovers, and Jessica's blushing embarrassment over her disguise.

GRATIANO

Gratiano seeks to elevate gaiety and exuberance into a philosophy of life, and in doing so becomes an object of ridicule. Festivity is one of the means by which the play frees itself from the cruel everyday world, making distinctions and observations about human behaviour in an atmosphere of joyous release; but, as an end in itself, jollity is shown to be merely vacuous. Gratiano tells Antonio that he takes life too seriously; he himself only wants to grow old laughing, drowning sadness in wine (I, i, 79–82). Inspired by Antonio's reserve, he deplores the sort of man who tries to appear wise by remaining silent (I, i, 88–99). This is hardly tactful, but no offence is taken, for although Gratiano is manifestly not the type of taciturn fool he describes, he is a fool nonetheless, speaking 'an infinite deal of nothing' (I, i, 114). Lorenzo's remark concerning Launcelot's wit could equally well have been inspired by Gratiano: 'I think the best grace of wit will shortly turn into silence, and discourse grow commendable in none only but parrots' (III, v, 40–42).

Certainly Gratiano's brand of wit is very laboured. A particularly poor example is contained in the trial scene. Watching Shylock whet his knife he observes (IV, i, 123–4):

> *Not on thy sole, but on thy soul, harsh Jew,*
> *Thou mak'st thy knife keen . . .*

Such humour is excruciating and draws a withering response from Shylock.

Gratiano is so 'wild . . . rude, and bold of voice' (II, ii, 168) that when he announces his engagement to Nerissa, Bassanio seems to doubt that his intentions can be honourable: 'And do you, Gratiano, mean good faith?' (III, ii, 210). He is indeed a rather unlikely lover. He shows a sign of tender affection for his wife when she rebukes him for parting with the ring she gave him, although his language retains his characteristic vulgarity (V, i, 144–5):

> *Would he were gelt that had it for my part,*
> *Since you do take it, love, so much at heart.*

However, displays of sentiment are clearly an effort for him and cannot be sustained. Portia inquires as to the subject of their quarrel, and he scorns the ring as a thing of little value, cruelly mocking its sentimental inscription.

Here Gratiano is more insensitive than vicious, but his conduct during Antonio's trial goes some way towards validating Shylock's contention that, in seeking revenge, he is only following the Christian example. He seems void of the 'quality of mercy' and thoroughly enjoys the final judgement on Shylock. His teasing echoes of Shylock's words in praise of Portia underline the comic symmetry of the scene, but also suggest a childish vindictiveness. Moreover, he employs the same expression as Shylock has used in his desire for revenge on Antonio. Shylock says, 'If I can catch him once upon the hip ...' (I, iii, 42), while Gratiano comes out with, 'Now, infidel, I have you on the hip!' (IV, i. 331).

It is a disturbing hint of a deep-rooted similarity in their characters. Gratiano warned that stubborn vengefulness would lead to damnation in his painful pun on 'sole' and 'soul', but unlike the Duke, he reveals precious little 'difference of ... spirit' (IV, i, 365). When Portia asks Antonio what mercy he can offer Gratiano interjects, 'A halter gratis! Nothing else, for God's sake!' (IV, i, 376).

Perhaps he should look to his own soul. He heightens our enjoyment of a comically satisfying poetic justice, but in the process seems to descend almost to Shylock's level.

SOLANIO AND SALERIO

These two young gallants are similar in more than name. Neither character is drawn in any depth: they are not intended to be individualized, but to typify the elegant, educated young gentlemen of the age. Their rich, eloquent language, mingling classical allusion with colourful colloquialism, sets the scene in Venice, a setting of cultured luxury and leisure. It is Salerio who first stresses the graceful social function of wealth in his elegant speech describing Antonio's argosies (I, i, 8–14), and the pair's refinement of word and manner forms a beautiful counterpoint to the vulgar, blustering Gratiano, and, more importantly, to Shylock's harsh austerity.

Often Solanio and Salerio are the servants of the plot. Salerio makes the first mention of Antonio's losses and also brings the letter confirming the worst to Bassanio in Belmont. However, they are also allowed to comment on the characters. They help to maintain the comic perspective on Shylock. Solanio gives an amusing rendition of Shylock's 'passion' on discovering the double loss of his daughter and his ducats, and is fond of the joke about Jews being devils (III, i, 19, 69), voicing the prejudices of a contemporary audience. They join together to tease him about his losses. In addition, Salerio highlights the contrast between Jessica and her father, and provides us with a moving eulogy of Antonio (II, viii, 35–49), clearly appreciating the quality of his sentiments. Displaying a tender concern for Antonio's sorrow, both Solanio and Salerio are in harmony with the play's ideals of love and friendship, as they grace the stage with their polished manners and eloquent speech.

LAUNCELOT GOBBO

The stage direction (Act II Scene ii) identifies Launcelot as 'the Clown', and he is the principal source of straightforward comedy in the play. He has not the status of the fool in the tragedy *King Lear*, where the jester's wit is matched by incisive intelligence and intense perception. We laugh as much at Launcelot as with him; his very appearance is ludicrous, with the comic appeal of the grotesque: *gobbo* in Italian means hunchbacked.

When we meet him for the first time he is alone, but the want of a butt for his wit cannot stem the stream of words: he is quite capable of supplying both sides of a dialogue, and a narrative to boot. He acts out an amusingly fiery debate between the 'fiend', who is urging him to leave Shylock, and his conscience, which advises him that his duty is to stay. It is an irreverent parody of the medieval tradition of quasi-dramatic dialogue on a moral theme. Here the moral becomes comically inverted, as Launcelot decides to obey the fiend, who 'gives the more friendly counsel' (I I, ii, 27).

Irreverence is a standard comic device, and Launcelot is very free with his insults. In this speech he declares that his father 'did something smack' [of lechery] and when Old Gobbo enters he amuses himself at some length at the old man's expense. He plays on his father's poor eyesight, refusing at first to admit his identity and telling him that his son is dead. This spectacle of youth teasing and baffling gullible old age is in a time-honoured tradition, but when Bassanio enters Launcelot is made to appear as foolish as his father. They are both equally pompous and long-winded, skirting around the subject without coming to the point of their business with Bassanio, which is that Launcelot wishes to join his service. Father and son come out with a torrent of malapropisms (such as we noted on p. 27), which only add to the comic confusion.

In this sort of word-play the joke is on Launcelot as an ignorant rustic (which the word 'clown' implies), but, as Lorenzo points out later, Launcelot has the characteristic talent for deliberate verbal witticism of a good fool (I I I, v, 56–9). He cleverly takes the sting out of Lorenzo's accusation that he has made the Negro pregnant, by punning skilfully on the words 'Moor' and 'more' (I I I, v, 36–8). He has 'an army of good words' at his disposal, and this exchange with Lorenzo is a good example of the purely verbal humour in the play, as Launcelot deliberately misconstrues and distorts the meaning of what is said to him, turning the plainest English into amusing nonsense (I I I, v, 33–59).

Because a clown is simultaneously an object of ridicule and a skilful comedian, Launcelot is the perfect vehicle for Shakespeare's exploitation of the comic appeal of the traditional stage Jew. Even a modern audience is able to laugh at his racist jibes about Shylock without feeling morally compromised, since Launcelot is himself often ludicrous and contemptible. So he trots out the standing jokes: 'the Jew is the very devil incarnation' (I I, ii, 24); he is also a miser, in whose service Launcelot is 'famished'; 'My master's a very Jew' (I I, ii, 97). He also mocks and teases Shylock to his face with rather more subtle

humour, goading him into an outburst of nervous anxiety about the
security and sobriety of his household by working on his superstitious
instincts (II, v, 22–6). Launcelot plays a part in maintaining our comic
perspective on Shylock, which is vital if he is not to attain tragic status.

The comic role of the clown thus has a structural function; moreover, Launcelot's jokes occasionally highlight important aspects of our
response to various characters. It is, after all, appropriate to stress
Shylock's meanness and wickedness. Similarly, when he teases Jessica
that she is 'damned' (III, v, 5), although we are unlikely to accept his
light-hearted explanation that 'the sins of the father are to be laid
upon the children' (a constant theme in Jewish theological history),
we recall our uneasiness about her own conduct in robbing and desert-
ing her father. Finally, Launcelot shows genuine understanding of
Bassanio's good qualities, cleverly dividing the proverb 'the grace of
God is gear enough' between his old and his new master. The latter
has the 'grace', Shylock has 'enough', that is, a competency in wealth
(II, ii, 138–40).

Launcelot can thus be perceptive, and he is not without some of
the qualities which we admire in Portia, Antonio and Bassanio. Shylock
describes him as an 'unthrifty knave' (I, iii, 172): he is careless of money,
and 'Snail-slow in profit' (II, v, 45). In addition, he shows considerable
affection and love for Jessica, shedding tears at their parting (II, iii, 10).
He remains a clown to the end, but is clearly the type of clown who
can be accommodated in Belmont.

Commentary

LOVE AND MONEY

The thriving merchant city of Venice was a prototype for London in the 1590s. Through trade, the English capital was becoming increasingly wealthy (even though most of the wealth was in the hands of a few). The cultured circles of its population were self-consciously aware of the wide-ranging effects of prosperity. On the one hand, riches could be regarded as a social blessing, bringing colour and the joy and release of festivity. On the other, increasing capital caused a growing unease about the power of money to corrupt, deprave and shatter social relations. *The Merchant of Venice* vividly portrays wealth in its conflicting roles; compares and contrasts it with the currency of love, and in the process articulates the need for an enlightened, liberal and, above all, social approach to money.

The play's opening immediately makes the association between riches and a decorous feeling for manners and colourful, civilized, structured society. For Salerio, Antonio's argosies (I, i, 10–14):

> *Like signors and rich burghers on the flood,*
> *Or as it were the pageants of the sea –*
> *Do overpeer the petty traffickers*
> *That curtsy to them, . . .*

Wealth is thus a gorgeous spectacle, a source of pleasure and the basis for graceful social relationships. Antonio has lent Bassanio large sums to support his opulent, gregarious lifestyle. In this way, money can be used for the sake of friendship, and Bassanio's latest venture provides the perfect opportunity for it to serve in affairs of the heart: one more loan will secure his friend's happiness by enabling him to win the hand of the woman he loves. It will also ensure that he is able to indulge his extravagant, festive temperament, for Portia has almost unlimited means. In the right hands money may thus be used to nurture love and contentment, to enrich the quality of life.

Generosity, that ability to give for love without thought of personal profit, is the ideal of the play. Portia also conforms to it well, joyfully giving herself and everything she owns to Bassanio, and declaring her willingness to pay his debt 'twenty times over' (III, ii, 307) in order to save his friend. For Portia money is only to be desired in so far as it can serve the cause of love. When Bassanio offers her the three thousand ducats meant to pay the debt, she declines because she considers Antonio's release sufficient reward: 'My mind was never yet more mercenary' (IV, i, 415). In this context of the celebration of happy liberality, where the value of money is kept in perspective, any form of extravagance is welcomed. So the prodigal Bassanio's dreams are realized, and the equally spendthrift Jessica, who spends 'Fourscore ducats at a sitting (III, i, 101) is similarly rewarded.

Against all this is set the coldly calculating character of Shylock. The usurer lends money for profit not love, and his destructive ability is clear: Antonio has had to rescue many victims of usury from total ruin (III, iii, 22–3). Shylock's exploitation of his wealth is the antithesis of Antonio's beneficence; he uses it not only for personal gain, but as a tool of his vindictiveness. He grants the loan and accepts Antonio's bond in order to 'catch him ... upon the hip', and 'feed fat' his 'ancient grudge' (I, iii, 43–4). His hatred is based on greed: for by his lending money without taking interest, Antonio has lowered the going rate for loans. So the viciousness and selfish greed of usury are contrasted with the love and generosity of lending out of Christian charity.

Shylock's depravity, therefore, is inextricably bound up with his obsession with money. He seems to have no conception of moral standards, judging people only by their financial resources. When he describes Antonio as a 'good man' (I, iii, 12) he is not implying that he is virtuous, only that he is wealthy. The study of the corrupting influence of Mammon in the character of Shylock comes to a peak in his reaction to Jessica's flight and the theft of his money and jewels. Avarice quashes natural feelings and humanity: he only wishes that his daughter were dead at his feet, with 'the ducats in her coffin' (III, i, 82).

Such are the sentiments of one who cares only for gold, ducats and precious stones. In Belmont, we discover a different currency. Bassanio and Portia constantly express their love in the imagery of financial transactions. He 'come[s] by note, to give and to receive' (III, ii, 140), and she wishes (III, ii, 156–9) that she

> ... *might in virtues, beauties, livings, friends,*
> *Exceed account; but the full sum of me*
> *Is sum of something, which, to term in gross,*
> *Is an unlessoned girl...*

This adoption of commercial language in a romantic context highlights the natural liberality of emotional attachments by encouraging the audience to think in terms of the business world. Moreover, it affirms the play's suggestions that money can be employed in the service of love.

However, the lovers' skill in the language of commerce also implies that they are implicated in the more unpleasant aspects of money. Portia describes her joy when Bassanio chooses the lead casket as an 'excess' (III, ii, 112), which is the word that Antonio had used to mean interest (I, iii, 59). It suggests that love has its own natural usury, but it is also a subtle reminder that even the romantic union of Belmont is not entirely free from the anything but romantic transactions of the money-lenders in Venice. Similarly, Antonio professes to be above usury but is forced to employ it. Bassanio rejects the silver casket which he sees as a symbol of money, but he has a financial motive in wooing Portia. No one, it seems, can remain completely untouched by Shylock's profiteering.

Antonio's, Bassanio's and Portia's manifest need for money is an ironic comment on the indifference which they sometimes affect towards it, but this irony does not put them on a level with Shylock. He wants money for its own sake; he worships Mammon and uses money for his own hateful purposes. The others desire wealth for the best of reasons, employing it in the service of friendship and festivity, both directing and subordinating it to love.

JUSTICE, MERCY AND THE LAW

In *The Merchant of Venice* a civilized society is shown to need the structure of an ordered existence within which to move. Flourishing trade is dependent on money, and complex social and business relations require recognized standards of conduct, formalized, and, if necessary, enforced by the law. So even in their horror at the cruel vengefulness of Shylock both Portia and Antonio stress the importance of justice being seen to be done. The Duke 'cannot deny the course of law' (III, iii, 26) because to do so would undermine the confidence of international traders that their transactions are governed and protected by the law. Similarly, Portia cannot abrogate an established decree, as it would be taken as a precedent (IV, i, 218–19),

> *And many an error by the same example*
> *Will rush into the state.*

Shylock understands and exploits this conviction: 'If you deny me, fie upon your law' (IV, i, 101). He knows that in demanding the grotesque forfeit of the bond he is only insisting on the principles of property on which their whole society is based. The Christians do what they like with their property, using their slaves 'in abject and in slavish parts,/Because [they] bought them'. He has paid for his pound of flesh, thus he may carve it off and do whatever he wants with it.

Just as Shylock loves money for its own sake rather than for its social value, he exploits the law as if it were an end in itself; he does not recognize it as the guiding principle of a harmonious, civilized life which it is intended to serve. He deprives it of all vestige of humanity, appealing only to the harsh prescription of dogma. So he demands that the exact wording of his legal contract be observed; the flesh must be cut from Antonio's breast: 'So says the bond' (IV, i, 250). He inverts the proper relationship between the law and society.—justice should be the servant of the community – but he tries to make the citizens of Venice the slaves and puppets of their own legal system. As Shylock sees it, the mere machinery of human life is exalted into an almost divine principle: his gods are Mammon and the law. Confidently secure in this narrow and blinkered existence, he has not the slightest suspicion of the broader interpretation of the law by which he will stand condemned: 'What judgement shall I dread, doing no wrong?' (IV, i, 89). Shylock has no concept of mercy.

He therefore supplies his judge with a plausible excuse for applying an equally literal interpretation of the law. Shylock has refused permission for a surgeon to stand by to tend Antonio because it is not a condition of the bond. But nor does the bond explicitly mention blood. So Shylock prepares the ground for Portia's legal quibble, which otherwise might seem but a cynical distortion of the law. Clearly, the mere letter of the law does not constitute absolute justice.

However, Portia's judgement is further sanctioned by the fact that, although she frustrates Shylock by manipulating the word of the law to suit her purpose, her motive for doing so is purely social. Her quibble does not emphasize the supremacy of legal terminology over people's lives, since it has as its basis a love for her husband and an admirable understanding of the sanctity of friendship. Justice is thus shown to exist in an application of the law conditioned by love. Unless the heart is the guiding principle, laws may simply be disruptive and be open to exploitation by the cruel and vindictive. In human affairs, then, it is a good thing that 'The brain may devise laws for the blood, but a hot temper leaps o'er a cold decree' (I, ii, 17–18). Love and emotions are the fulfilment of the law.

In this way Portia subjugates rigorous legal compulsion to a broader and more enlightened concept of justice, and appeals to principles such as mercy which cannot be formally provided for in statutes. When she says that Shylock must be merciful (IV, i, 179), she knows that her words do not have the force of law (IV, i, 181–3):

> *The quality of mercy is not strained;*
> *It droppeth as the gentle rain from heaven*
> *Upon the place beneath.*

Mercy is thus an 'attribute to God' (IV, i, 192), and Portia stresses the fallacy of Shylock's attitude that right and wrong begin and end in obeying human law (IV, i, 195–7):

> *Though justice be thy plea, consider this:*
> *That in the course of justice none of us*
> *Should see salvation.*

The clash between Shylock and Portia in the trial is to some extent a conflict between the doctrine of the Old and New Testaments. In the opinion of Shakespeare's contemporaries, the Jewish people lived by strict adherence to the harsh laws of the Old Testament. Christians, on the other hand, had a more humane ideal, based on the law of love which Christ had brought them. Shylock, being a Jew, has no understanding of Christian mercy and love. Portia, in her famous trial speech, shows that the law can be harmful if it is not illuminated by the love and mercy which her extrovert Christian temperament so obviously shows.

However, the play is concerned with social rather than theological problems. Portia's humanity is set against Shylock's dogmatism; the close-knit Venetian community against an egoistical alien. Shylock is not part of a tolerant way of life which is governed more by bonds of friendship than by legal contracts.

The tolerance which harmonizes the justice meted out by the Christians is to be admired, although it is rather less sublime than the mercy which drops like rain from heaven. Shylock is forced to beg for mercy (IV, i, 361) and although he appears to be released from the severest material penalties, he must suffer the pain and humiliation of a forced conversion to Christianity, and the legal recognition of Lorenzo, the hated representative of that religion who has eloped with his daughter. As in the play's examination of economic morality, so in its study of justice, abstract standards of perfection do not seem to be within the scope of human beings. Nonetheless a healthy distinction is drawn between different ways of applying the law, and once again the touchstones of judgement are the values of community and love.

DECEPTION AND DISGUISE

The difference between appearance and reality is a constant theme in Shakespearean drama. In *The Merchant of Venice* it is an important aspect of the development of plot and character both in the story of the bond, which unfolds in Venice, and in the tale of the caskets, set in Belmont.

Shylock's affected 'kindness' (I, iii, 140) in proposing the terms of his loan immediately illustrates the necessity for the characters to detect deception, and the dangers inherent in a superficial assessment of temperament and motives. Earlier in the scene, Antonio has shown that he is aware of the need for incisive judgement: 'O what a goodly outside falsehood hath!' (I, iii, 99). Nonetheless he unfortunately proceeds to accept the 'merry bond' (I, iii, 69) at face value, thinking that Shylock 'grows kind' (I, iii, 174). Bassanio is less confident: 'I like not fair terms and a villain's mind' (I, iii, 176).

The ability to look below the surface and perceive true values (or vices) is exactly what the test of the caskets is designed for. Morocco learns that 'All that glisters is not gold' (II, vii, 65), and Arragon is sped on his way with a maxim on the same theme (II, ix, 69–70):

> *There be fools alive iwis,*
> *Silvered o'er, and so was this.*

Bassanio, who, on the other hand, appeared to see through Shylock's hypocrisy, shows by his lengthy deliberation that he is not one of these 'fools'. 'The world is still deceived with ornament', which hides 'grossness' even in religion, a reminder of the way that Shylock manipulates scriptural texts. 'Supposed fairness', then, is (III, ii, 100–101):

> *The seeming truth which cunning times put on*
> *To entrap the wisest.*

Bassanio is successful simply because he refuses to judge by appearances (III, ii, 131–2):

> *You that choose not by the view*
> *Chance as fair, and choose as true.*

This idea is illuminated many times in the course of the play. For instance, Lorenzo perceives the qualities he associates with Christians in his Jewish lover, for as Jessica points out: 'though I am a daughter to his [Shylock's] blood,/I am not to his manners'. (II, iii, 18–19). Again, Launcelot's comic discourse (II, ii, 1–28) touches on the same theme: his conscience should offer the best advice, but, on close examination, the fiend is really offering 'the more friendly counsel'.

The happiness attained by these characters at the close of the play comes about through this ability to see beyond superficial appearances. For Bassanio and Lorenzo, in particular, it is the reward for perceiving beauty in virtue and love, not merely in ornament, physical appearance, or the circumstances of birth, which may be misleading.

Yet the play's happy ending is also dependent on a benevolent form of deception which the characters do not detect. The blissful harmony of the final Act would be impossible without the artfulness of Portia in her disguise as the doctor of law. Her pretence is entirely constructive. It is like the artifice of the author, making use of the devices available in a comedy to save Antonio from the knife, and his friends from heartbreak. In the scene concerning the ring, it preserves Gratiano and Bassanio from disloyalty, as they unwittingly give away the symbols of their fidelity to their own wives in disguise.

However, it is vital to realize that while the characters are completely taken in by Portia's deception, the audience is not. We are fully aware of the outrageous disguise and scheming which lie behind the contrived outcome of the trial. So, just as Bassanio has seen through the dull casing of the lead casket to find his heart's desire, so the audience can perceive the love and social feeling embodied in Portia beneath the appearances of her legal attire and her pedantic legal quibbling. Moreover, by highlighting the disguise and artifice involved in averting disaster for Antonio and his friends, Shakespeare warns his audience not to take the play's comic, happy ending too literally, and not to consider that the distinctions made in the play are intended to form a strict and practical code of ethics.

Discussion Topic and Examination Questions

Your understanding and appreciation of the play will be much increased if you discuss it with other people. Here are some topics you could consider:

1. 'In sooth I know not why I am so sad!' Solanio and Salerio found it difficult to explain Antonio's melancholy. What is your view of it?

2. Consider the use of disguise and deception and their place in the play.

3. The stories of the three caskets and the pound of flesh are both remote from reality. Do we take them seriously in the play and, if so, why?

4. It has been said that Venice and Belmont represent two quite different attitudes to life. Explore this idea and its effect on our understanding of the play.

5. People often feel sorry of Shylock. Is there any justification for this?

6. Do you feel that modern attitudes may make us regard the play in a different light from the audience of Shakespeare's time?

7. This play has a good deal to say about money and business affairs. Collect as many examples of this as you can and discuss their overall effect on human relationships in the play.

8. Shakespeare removes Shylock – the most striking character – from the play at the end of Act IV. Why do you think he did this?

THE GCSE EXAMINATION

If you are studying for the GCSE examination, you may find that the set texts have been selected by your teacher from a very wide list of suggestions in the examination syllabus. The questions in the examination paper will therefore be applicable to many different books and plays. Here are some possible questions which you could answer by making use of *The Merchant of Venice*:

1. Much has been written about characters who are in some ways different from the society in which they live. Discuss such a character from a book or play you know, outlining the situation and how he or she reacts to it.

In your opinion, does each of the principal characters get what he or she deserves by the end of the play? (You may confine your remarks to three characters only, if you wish.)

2. To what extent do you feel that 'the quality of mercy' is shown at the end of the trial scene and has justice been done?

3. What can you find to criticize in the behaviour and attitudes of Antonio, Bassanio and Jessica?

4.   Distinguish between the characters of Portia's three suitors – Morocco, Arragon and Bassanio – and explain the reasons that led each to his choice of casket.

5.   Sinister, comic, tragic – how far are these words useful in describing Shylock?

6.   Discuss the part each of the following played in *The Merchant of Venice*: Gratiano, Launcelot, Gobbo, Lorenzo.

7.   Compare and contrast the attitudes of Bassanio, Portia and Shylock towards wealth and its uses.

(c) Give the meaning of the following lines and say why Portia makes this comment:

'To offend and judge are distinct offices
And of opposed natures.'   (ll. 26–7)

(d) State the inscriptions on the other two caskets, and give the substance of Arragon's comments on them.

(e) What do we learn of Arragon's character from the passage and from his previous comments? State your evidence.

(*University of London Examination Board, 1980*)

13. Read the following passage, and answer all the questions printed beneath it:

SALERIO

My wind, cooling my broth,
Would blow me to an ague, when I thought
What harm a wind too great might do at sea.
I should not see the sandy hour-glass run
But I should think of shallows and of flats,   5
And see my wealthy Andrew dock'd in sand
Vailing her high-top lower than her ribs
To kiss her burial. Should I go to church
And see the holy edifice of stone,
And not bethink me straight of dangerous rocks,   10
Which touching but my gentle vessel's side
Would scatter all her spices on the stream,
Enrobe the roaring waters with my silks;
And, in a word, but even now worth this,
And now worth nothing? Shall I have the thought   15
To think on this, and shall I lack the thought
That such a thing bechanc'd would make me sad?
But tell not me: I know Antonio
Is sad to think upon his merchandise.

ANTONIO

    Believe me, no: I thank my fortune for it,   20

    My ventures are not in one bottom trusted,

    Nor to one place; nor is my whole estate

    Upon the fortune of this present year:

    Therefore, my merchandise makes me not sad.

SALERIO

    Why, then you are in love.

ANTONIO   Fie, fie!   25

SALERIO

    Not in love neither? Then let's say you are sad,

    Because you are not merry: and 'twere as easy

    For you to laugh and leap, and say you are merry,

    Because you are not sad. Now, by two-headed Janus,

    Nature hath fram'd strange fellows in her time: 30

    Some that will evermore peep through their eyes

    And laugh like parrots at a bag-piper,

    And other of such vinegar aspect

    That they'll not show their teeth in way of smile,

    Though Nestor swear the jest be laughable.   35

   (*i*) Explain: *wealthy Andrew* (l.6); *Vailing her ... her burial* (ll. 7–8); and *two-headed Janus* (l.29).

   (*ii*) What do you think might be the reason for Antonio's state of mind here?

   (*iii*) What are the main topics touched upon in this extract? What is their significance in relation to the play as a whole?

               (*University of Oxford Examination Board, 1982*)

FOR THE BEST IN PAPERBACKS, LOOK FOR THE 🐧

In every corner of the world, on every subject under the sun, Penguin represents quality and variety – the very best in publishing today.

For complete information about books available from Penguin – including Puffins, Penguin Classics and Arkana – and how to order them, write to us at the appropriate address below. Please note that for copyright reasons the selection of books varies from country to country.

In the United Kingdom: Please write to *Dept E.P., Penguin Books Ltd, Harmondsworth, Middlesex, UB7 0DA*.

If you have any difficulty in obtaining a title, please send your order with the correct money, plus ten per cent for postage and packaging, to *PO Box No 11, West Drayton, Middlesex*

In the United States: Please write to *Dept BA, Penguin, 299 Murray Hill Parkway, East Rutherford, New Jersey 07073*

In Canada: Please write to *Penguin Books Canada Ltd, 2801 John Street, Markham, Ontario L3R 1B4*

In Australia: Please write to the *Marketing Department, Penguin Books Australia Ltd, P.O. Box 257, Ringwood, Victoria 3134*

In New Zealand: Please write to the *Marketing Department, Penguin Books (NZ) Ltd, Private Bag, Takapuna, Auckland 9*

In India: Please write to *Penguin Overseas Ltd, 706 Eros Apartments, 56 Nehru Place, New Delhi, 110019*

In the Netherlands: Please write to *Penguin Books Netherlands B.V., Postbus 195, NL–1380AD Weesp*

In West Germany: Please write to *Penguin Books Ltd, Friedrichstrasse 10–12, D–6000 Frankfurt/Main 1*

In Spain: Please write to *Longman Penguin España, Calle San Nicolas 15, E–28013 Madrid*

In Italy: Please write to *Penguin Italia s.r.l., Via Como 4, I-20096 Pioltello (Milano)*

In France: Please write to *Penguin Books Ltd, 39 Rue de Montmorency, F-75003 Paris*

In Japan: Please write to *Longman Penguin Japan Co Ltd, Yamaguchi Building, 2-12-9 Kanda Jimbocho, Chiyoda-Ku, Tokyo 101*

FOR THE BEST IN PAPERBACKS, LOOK FOR THE 🐧

PENGUIN SELF-STARTERS

Self-Starters are designed to help you develop skills and proficiency in the subject of your choice. Each book has been written by an expert and is suitable for school-leavers, students, those considering changing their career in mid-stream and all those who study at home.

Titles published or in preparation:

Accounting	Noel Trimming
Acting	Nigel Rideout
Advertising	Michael Pollard
Basic Statistics	Peter Gwilliam
Business Communication	Doris Wheatley
A Career in Banking	Sheila Black, John Brennan
Clear English	Vivian Summers
Fashion and Design	Ken Baynes, Krysia Brochocka, Beverly Saunders
Five-Hour Keyboarding Course	Madeleine Brearley
Job-Hunting	Alfred Hossack
Marketing	Marsaili Cameron, Angela Rushton, David Carson
Nursing	David White
Personnel Management	J. D. Preston
Public Relations	Sheila Black, John Brennan
Public Speaking	Vivian Summers
Report Writing	Doris Wheatley
Retailing	David Couch
Secretarial Skills	Gail Cornish, Charlotte Coudrille, Joan Lipkin-Edwardes
Starting a Business on a Shoestring	Michel Syrett, Chris Dunn
Typing	Gill Sugden

FOR THE BEST IN PAPERBACKS, LOOK FOR THE 🐧

PENGUIN CRITICAL STUDIES

Described by *The Times Educational Supplement* as 'admirable' and 'superb', Penguin Critical Studies is a specially developed series of critical essays on the major works of literature for use by students in universities, colleges and schools.

titles published or in preparation include:

FOR THE BEST IN PAPERBACKS, LOOK FOR THE 🐧

PENGUIN CRITICAL STUDIES

Described by *The Times Educational Supplement* as 'admirable' and 'superb', Penguin Critical Studies is a specially developed series of critical essays on the major works of literature for use by students in universities, colleges and schools.

titles published or in preparation include:

SHAKESPEARE
Antony and Cleopatra
As You Like It
Henry IV Part 2
Henry V
Julius Caesar
King Lear
Macbeth
Measure for Measure
Much Ado About Nothing
Richard II
Richard III
Romeo and Juliet
A Shakespeare Handbook
Shakespeare's History Plays
Shakespeare – Text into Performance
The Tempest
Troilus and Cressida
Twelfth Night
A Winter's Tale

CHAUCER
A Chaucer Handbook
The Miller's Tale
The Nun's Priest's Tale
The Pardoner's Tale
The Prologue to the Canterbury
  Tales

FOR THE BEST IN PAPERBACKS, LOOK FOR THE 🐧

PENGUIN PASSNOTES

This comprehensive series, designed to help GCSE students, includes:

SUBJECTS
Biology
Chemistry
Economics
English Language
Geography
Human Biology
Mathematics
Nursing
Oral English
Physics

SHAKESPEARE
As You Like It
Henry IV Part I
Henry V
Julius Caesar
Macbeth
The Merchant of Venice
A Midsummer Night's Dream
Romeo and Juliet
Twelfth Night

LITERATURE
Across the Barricades
The Catcher in the Rye
Cider with Rosie
The Crucible
Death of a Salesman
Far From the Madding Crowd
Great Expectations
Gregory's Girl
I am the Cheese
I'm the King of the Castle
The Importance of Being Earnest
Jane Eyre
Joby
Journey's End
Kes
Lord of the Flies
A Man for All Seasons
The Mayor of Casterbridge
My Family and Other Animals
Oliver Twist
The Pardoner's Tale
Pride and Prejudice
The Prologue to the Canterbury
  Tales
Pygmalion
Roots
The Royal Hunt of the Sun
Silas Marner
A Taste of Honey
To Kill a Mockingbird
Wuthering Heights
Z for Zachariah